A STORY OF HOPE

YEARS &
SIX MONTHS

ERIKA L. ORRISS

TWENTY YEARS & SIX MONTHS

A Story of Hope

Copyright © 2023. Erika Orriss.

Book Design by Transcendent Publishing
P.O. Box 66202
St. Pete Beach, FL 33736

ISBN: 979-8-9878728-9-5

Printed in the United States of America.

Dedication

To my children, Jessica and Jonathan, who were my constant source of inspiration to fight on even when I felt like dying. They were not going to grow up without a mother if I could do anything about it.

Table of Contents

Author's Note

Every book requires a spark of inspiration before it can be birthed. I also believe it takes a catalyst, something or someone who pushes the author to act on that inspiration. Though many supported and encouraged me, it was my children, Jessica and Jonathan, who inspired me to write this book. Jessica, now twenty-eight, served as a catalyst as she expressed a desire to have a record of our experiences to pass to her own children when the time comes. Both Jessica and Jonathan suffered as a result of my illness, though in different ways. They have also gained strength of character in many ways.

Jessica had known a mom who took her on hikes in the woods. For a while it was just the two of us, before I met my husband, and she thought I walked on water. She and I were very close and did everything together. I'm sure my illness was surreal for her. One day I was taking her ice skating and the next, or so it seemed, I was painted out of her everyday life. No more spelling quizzes on the ride to school; in fact, no more rides to school, at least from Mom.

My son, Jonathan, was four-and-a-half years younger and we tried to shield him from the brunt of it. At the age of two and a half, who knew how much he could comprehend? His only understanding was that Mommy wasn't there for bedtime stories, hugging him when he was scared, and late-night snacks. Mom was gone. What was going through his head? *My Mommy is gone, and I need her. Please come back soon.* For him, there was no explanation, just loss.

At first my husband tried telling him I was on a business trip. Jessica obviously was too quick for this; at the ripe old age of six she wanted the real story. Jonathan tried to believe his dad but eventually would catch on that it was no business trip.

I am not sure which got the worst of it. Furthermore, does it matter? There is no way to compare pain.

For many years I was plagued with relentless guilt about what they went through. However, I eventually realized that guilt blocks us from being of any real value to anyone.

If I wanted to effectively help people I had to set that guilt down, and doing so has been part of my journey. I sincerely hope that in sharing my story I can help others understand that whatever challenges they are going through, there is always hope.

Introduction

My name is Erika Orriss. I am your typical mom, the lady standing next to you in line at the grocery store. And if you saw me in the store, you would never know the hell I have lived through or the continued struggles from this illness that have plagued me through the years. I now work as a licensed mental health counselor helping others deal with life-altering events, but this is my personal journey that started the change of my life, and my outlook, forever.

I have not always been a counselor. For many years I was a successful software engineer, and that's what I was doing when I fell ill out of the blue. We had to google the diagnosis: Guillain-Barre Syndrome, is a rare neurological illness. What was happening? I had not planned on this. Who plans on this? Life fell apart, and fast. I had to rebuild it in a completely different way. This is once it was determined I was going to live.

Too sick to work, I went back to grad school so I didn't go stir-crazy as I waited patiently for my body to come back from this rare neurological illness. I had always wanted to help others, and here was a chance. I have another chance in writing this book. It seeks to answer the question: *How do we manage and live on when the unimaginable happens?*

I had not originally intended on writing to help those with rare diseases (although I know many who suffer in silence and would love to give a voice to them), or those who have gone through overwhelming life events; it was meant for my children, who had been too young to understand. However, as I began writing I knew it was a story that needed to be told.

While this book does raise awareness of a rare disease and how to keep going, my hope is that it helps anyone suffering from a catastrophic event. Sometimes just hearing someone else's story of relentless suffering brings ease because it lets us know we are not alone.

Life can change on a dime. It is frightening how quickly we can go from the neighbor next door raising kids, working full-time to a statistic is alarming. Our perception and handling of these events is often a gift, although it never feels like it at the time. Many times, I wanted to die. Many times, I wanted to give up. Other times I got so mad. I was absolutely enraged and that may have been what enabled me to keep fighting (along with a lot of support and lots of people praying for me).

As mentioned, this book encompasses my journey through Guillain-Barre Syndrome (GBS). GBS is quite rare. According to the Center for Disease Control, just three to six thousand people in the United States will develop it each year. GBS can cause the entire body to become paralyzed; however, in most cases it does not cause the entire body to become paralyzed. For most folks, they do not require ventilation. That is not my story, at one point even my eye was paralyzed and had to be taped shut. I was on a ventilator for four months. I was not expected to live and told to prepare for the inevitable. My mother drove around with a black dress in her trunk for nearly six months.

Instead, my husband brought me back into the hospital the following Christmas with an Apple Pie for the ICU nurses, we all cried. I was a miracle; I remain a miracle. My husband never gave up. My kids never gave up, I am so grateful for all the support and love I received. I feel these components of recovery are every bit as important as the surgeons' hands and good medical care.

This is a story full of miracles. It is a story of family, love, determination, and the will to survive against all odds. It was definitely the grace of God carrying me through, but I had to bring a shovel. It wasn't always pretty. In fact, most of the time it was dark and bleak. Life isn't always pretty; however, sometimes in our darkest times we have our finest hour.

This is my story of hope. We can walk through anything, even paralyzed. So, walk on.

Chapter 1

A Narrative
(Gotta Start Somewhere)

I could do anything I set my mind to do – at least that is what I was told often and from a very young age by my father. He was very strong-willed, had lived a very hard life, and moved up and on to create his best life possible. Suffice it to say, by all appearances he was right! I went from being made fun of by our country club swim team as I tried to swim butterfly (the other children called me "Moth" due to my inability to lift my arms out of the water) to setting the state record by spring of the next year.

Mind you, it was not a natural ability; it was the result of pure determination and dedication. My older sister was born truly exceptional, while I had to work for everything I got. However, I did work, and I achieved whatever I set my mind to do, as my father had told me.

When I was nineteen my father was diagnosed with cancer. By the time I was twenty-two, Dad who was just fifty-one, had lost his battle and I had lost my biggest cheerleader.

I was in my senior year of college at the time, and my father suffered a major stroke the week before my final exams. The end was near and I knew I needed to fly out and see him. On the other hand, I also knew it would break his heart if I didn't graduate that semester. Though it was difficult to wait, I decided it would be much better than seeing him without the degree. I took my senior finals with the suitcase under my bed awaiting the call.

I appreciate my father for instilling in me such drive, dedication, and determination. Of course, at age twenty I didn't appreciate having to take care of him when my peers were partying in Florida for spring break; I also wasn't even sure I wanted to go to college at all. We had a special bond, and I just couldn't disappoint him. But that is all for another book.

I am no stranger to illness. I watched my father go from a world-renowned professor with a doctorate in neuropsychology getting his dream job in California to a dying man. He did not die immediately, though. He took that dream job, which quickly became too much for him. Still, in the short time he worked there he did accomplish a great deal, including an overhaul of their budget that saved the school many thousands of dollars.

He deteriorated over the next several years, eventually having the stroke that rendered him paralyzed on one side, unable to talk, and hospitalized for months before he died. The unimaginable had happened. Our family had become a statistic just like I would years later when I lay in the hospital bed at Orlando Regional Medical Center. Only when I was in the bed, I felt rage!

Of course, there were many events in between – many of them good (some not so good). However, I really built a good life for myself and I worked for it.

Childhood aside, my dad's death had been hard, and I drank to deal with it.

My twenties had been a struggle. I did manage to get a degree in computer science while dealing with my feelings of grief and loss over my father's illness and ultimate passing. However, upon graduation I could barely hold a job at the garbage factory in Newark to sustain my rented room.

Things were not easy in those early years after Dad's death, but I turned it around with the help of people who loved me when I didn't love myself. I learned how to snow ski, play guitar, and sing, and I had a lot of fun living above a hairdresser in Garfield, New Jersey, about a half-hour from New York City. Later, I decided to move to the western part of the state. I was still working in my field at AT&T and still a half-hour drive to work, but now I was surrounded by beautiful mountains and quaint small towns. I loved it there. I grew a garden and was closer to ski resorts in Pennsylvania.

I was thrilled (not to mention a little nervous) when at twenty-nine I became pregnant with my little Jessica. I was also very surprised. I never dreamed that my body could handle a pregnancy or that God would give me the opportunity.

I had this beautiful baby who looked just like her dad, *oh my goodness*. He had taken off the minute I found out that I was pregnant and planned on keeping her. I didn't care. I listened to lullabies with her every night and thanked God for His favor in my life. I felt incredibly blessed, and those blessings kept coming.

While pregnant I had met an amazing man who loved both of us. He went to Lamaze classes with me and was at my side during Jessica's birth. He was and probably still is an amazing man. *(He even came to check on me when I was sick with GBS and helped with the kids.)* Ultimately, though, we were on different paths, meaning I wanted more of a traditional family that included marriage and more children, and he did not. After a couple of years of hoping he would come around, I had to let him go, and that is when Dale Orriss walked into my life. He was kind and loved Jessica. He also had three children of his own from a previous marriage. We got along well. His very type B personality was a perfect complement to my overly type A. I got things done and he kept the peace.

A year after our first date we were married at a lovely ceremony in which all the kids took part. Shortly after that, we welcomed our beautiful son, Jonathan, into our family. We hit some rough patches in the early years, for sure. Unfortunately, Dale's children moved to Arizona, and I was offered a wonderful job in Florida (where I had always wanted to be). Money was tight, so Dale wanted to stay in New Jersey for a while and make some more before coming down, but the truth was, we were struggling as a couple.

When I told my mom I was moving to Florida, she told me I was crazy, probably because I had a broken wrist, a marriage on the rocks, a sick baby, and a stubborn spoiled four-year-old.

"It's impossible," Mom said, to which I replied, "Watch me."

Six months later we were in a new home in Orlando, Florida. I was working for Darden Corporation as a project manager and loving it.

I wasn't quite sure when Dale wanted to come down, or if I even wanted him to. I was doing it!! I was tired and overworked, but doing it!! I felt very lucky.

Dale came down about nine months later and we settled in together. It turned out to be a good decision. We had our arguments, but we settled. My career was taking off and the kids were good. We lived in a brand-new house that I had designed with the builder. Life was good!

Jessica was into ice skating, and we took her often for lessons and performances. The rink had "family days," and we all skated; then one day I tried to show off and fell and broke my wrist (Yes, I broke it again, this time very badly.) It was that year that I got a persistent stomach bug as well, becoming violently ill about every three months. It was very strange. I also quit diet soda cold turkey right before Thanksgiving.

I would later learn that while these events were unrelated, the combination could have caused the immune system to malfunction and potentially triggered Guillain-Barre Syndrome. Additionally, I caught an upper respiratory infection that I could not shake. I went to the clinic at Darden, and they filled me with antibiotics. My back hurt too, and I wasn't sure what was happening. Neither was anyone else, as even when the infection seemed to have gone away, I felt awful. I kept calling in sick and leaving early (very unlike me). One nurse practitioner said I "had a cold" in my back – this is when I realized they were lost.

One afternoon, I was so sick and terrified that I left work early, stopped by Dale's job and told him I thought something was terribly wrong. He said to go home and rest and we would figure it out, but by that night I could barely walk. I was staggering to the bathroom and taking warm baths. Warm baths were my only relief.

Christmas came and it was beautiful, but I had to lay back down. I had never needed to lay back down in my whole adult life (Dale used to tell me I had a "double-A" personality!). I told Dale I felt like I had been hit by a bus! I didn't understand what was happening. My condition was up and down that holiday season, but on New Year's night I couldn't lift the ham into the oven. I started crawling around on the floor to get around. And still, we had no answers.

On January 3, 2001, I awoke and told Dale I was sick, very sick. I didn't know what was wrong. He said to get an appointment later in the day and he could go with me. He was very good that way. I called the doctor at 9 a.m. when they opened, and they said they had an opening at 2:30. I informed the receptionist that I could be dead by that time. She said to come in right away.

I always wore fancy beautiful shoes but this time my feet hurt, and I had a strange sensation in them. I pulled out my old Reeboks and tried to walk in them. I was tripping so much that I decided for safety's sake to sit in the living room and wait for Dale.

By the time I got to the doctor's I was vomiting in the flowerbeds of the office and could not carry my own weight. The doctor asked if I had been sick recently and I said I'd had an upper respiratory infection. He said I was probably dehydrated and that I could either go home and drink a lot of fluids or go to the hospital. I almost screamed "Hospital!" but I was too weak. By this time, it took three people to hold up my one-hundred-five-pound body and get me to the car.

Again, that was January 3, 2001. By January 9, I would be on life support, and I would not leave the hospital until June 9. My life was going to be forever changed.

Chapter 2

The Journey Begins

ithout a doubt, the choice to go to Orlando Regional Medical Center rather than home (to drink a lot of fluids) was one of the best I've ever made. I didn't realize it then, though. At that moment I was confused and fearful for my job.

By evening my legs were burning and had stabbing pain so bad I was screaming at all the nurses. I, who had gone without any drugs (including alcohol) of any kind for thirteen years, was clamoring for them.

"Someone help me!" I screamed. "I can't walk! Something's wrong! Get help!"

They didn't know what to do either.

I think someone finally gave me some pain meds so I could fake it somewhat when Dale brought the kids in to see me. Dale had promised the kids I'd be home that evening and later told Jonathan that I was on a business trip. We didn't know what to say to them. Jonathan, who was just two-and-a-half, didn't understand much other than that I wasn't there, but for six-year-old Jessica it was worse. She wanted to know why I wasn't home. Six weeks would pass before I saw my darling children again. Now I will invite you into my private journey, not quite on a daily basis, but close enough.

As I open the journal and wipe off the dust, I do not see the initial entries I made. I see a couple of pages with entries from a year later, perhaps when I started this journey of remembering. For a long time, I was unable to write. I was just so angry and determined to go to as much therapy as possible to get better that NOTHING else in my world mattered. I continued with physical therapy long after it was prescribed. I paid for it myself and I never missed an appointment. I was going to get my life back, damn it! And I guess I did, but it's been a very long road. Here are a couple of entries I wrote shortly after I returned home from the hospital and was trying to piece together all I had been through.

July ?, 2002

My memories. My God, I lived through some sort of nightmare and in many ways, I am still living it. Perhaps that has been my hesitation to write. Like, somehow, just let me get better first.

It was over for everyone else long before it was for me. I still struggle with therapy and trying to engage in all sorts of other physical activity to improve my feet, my balance, my walking, et cetera.

Still using the Tens unit. I use the stupid electrodes every night but at least it's not 2x a day anymore!!

July 22, 2002

Got rid of the wheelchair today, praise God!!

My physical therapy ran out again so I'm back @ CORA.

Jimmy (a physical therapist assistant) says my left foot looks better but I walk like I'm raising my hips. *Oh, great,* I think.

I'm sick of this today and I look like a grandmother – just great!!

(*I was so sickly and old-looking that someone at a store asked if I was Jonathan's grandmother. Broke my heart.)

August 2002

To remember the events…God, can I recall the torment? The nights of endless minutes and listening to the ventilator, frightened to death. Would I live or would I die tonight? The blackness that was my life every night.

I remember the commotion outside my room and the silence of only the humming and compressing of the ventilator in my room.

Gosh, I don't know if I can write my experiences. How did I live through them? How do I live today? I plan every step. I must as I may lose motor control from the damage done to my nerves. My feet have completely abnormal sensations, as if I always have a boot on. As the day wears on I feel stabbing pain up my legs from my feet. Every night at dinner I pray to God that He will heal my feet.

The initial entries of the journal were awkward and difficult, but I did continue to write. Much of this book is taken directly from the daily journal entries because that's how I lived it – day to day, minute to minute, and at times, second to second.

I also rely heavily on my mother's notes and journals, which I can't thank her enough for keeping. Her dates of procedures and outings are much more accurate than mine and were immensely helpful as I wrote this book.

Of course, Mom's journal is written from her perspective. I was the one in the bed. And while it is hard for everyone, the caretakers can get up and go for a walk. The folks in the bed have an immensely different experience and most don't tell of it. There are a couple of books by others who had survived, and reading them helped me. I would devour those books. It felt like a secret club that most didn't understand, but we, the people in the bed, we got it. It gave me so much strength to push on.

Chapter 3

The Early Days

January 2, 2001

$\mathcal{F}$eeling sick – like someone ran me over with a bus. So unlike me to feel so sick and so tired. I feel tired beyond repair.

Tomorrow I'll be off to work, can't miss that. I've got two kids to support. Besides I like to work. I like feeling productive. I love how it feels at the end of the day when I've done all I could at work and for my family. I like my life. I had a period of marital problems, but besides that I am pretty happy. I feel satisfied. After years of striving for a good life I finally feel complete, and life makes sense.

This past Christmas was the first that I actually got all my presents off on time!! Mom thought I was working too hard, but I loved it!! I had Christmas at my house with my family and mom and stepfather, Ron, as usual. It was great, except that I was so tired on Christmas day, I had to take a nap. So weird for me.

January 2, 2001

I am not feeling right. I wake up all night with strange pain in my feet and legs. I make it to the garden tub (my beautiful tub that I barely ever use) and sit in the hot water. This helps some.

I go to work, but my back hurts and I am getting frustrated with all these physical distractions. I ask Lisa (my boss) if I can go to our Wellness Center (I work at Darden Restaurants). I felt so guilty doing so because I know there is much work to do and don't like to complain. Lisa says, "Fine" from beneath her busy desk, and I wander off half limping.

At the Wellness Center I am seen by a pretty physician's assistant who guesses I have a cold in my back. She gives me some Skelaxin (muscle relaxer) and says to go home early.

Feeling like a big baby, I left around 3:00. Then, after telling Dale to get the kids, I go home and straight to sleep.

January 3, 2001 – BAD DAY

I awake after another bad night's sleep. Something is wrong (*a phrase that will haunt me for the next twenty years*) I tell Dale that I'm staying home from work, then call Lisa and let her know as well. I still hurt and think I need rest.

At 9 a.m. I awake again. Something is very wrong. I can't feel my feet. I am lying in bed and can barely reach for the phone. I must see a doctor at once. I am so weak. The doctor's office says he can't see me until 2:30, to which I reply I don't think I will make it that long. They then fit me in at 9:30, which is great but means I now have to rush, which is not easy. I try to walk but it feels like I am walking on air (and not in a good way). My coordination is way off and I am so weak. I call Dale to ask him to come and get me and take me to the doctor. His response is classic: "Erika, this had better be good!" He is frustrated by the short notice and about missing more work (he has missed a lot during the previous year due to my stomach bugs).

I am falling up the stairs. Now I am scared – what the hell is happening?! I grab my shoes, then think again and trade them in for my good old Reeboks. I am normally not a tennis shoe girl but these are definitely not normal circumstances.

Carefully I make my way downstairs to wait for Dale. I sit in the living room chair, afraid to go anywhere else. I thank God when he arrives. He helps load me into the car. I am telling him to hurry up as we are late and they squeezed us in.

We are headed down Orange Avenue when I begin to feel nauseous. Dale reaches over and puts the car seat back for me. I think I'll vomit before I make it there. I just try to hang on.

Aaah – we have made it. I need help getting out of the car and help to stand. I vomit in the flowerbeds at the doctor's office entranceway, but we have made it.

They take one look at me and rush me through. The doctor checks my eyes, ears, et cetera. He asks me if I've been sick and I tell him I had a flu – or rather an upper respiratory infection – over Christmas. He shrugs his shoulders and says I must be dehydrated – would I like to go home and drink a lot, or go to the hospital to get intravenous hydration? Mind you, I am falling over. I can't stand on my own, and Dale and two nurses have to hold me up so I can get back to the waiting room to check out.

I don't believe that I am dehydrated, but since I'm no doctor I agree to go to the hospital for intravenous hydration. The doctor has pushed it, saying the hospital will have me feeling better faster and perhaps I can even make it into work in the afternoon.

Part of me feels like I am just wasting space at this hospital and am embarrassed as I call Lisa to give her an update. Dale goes back to work; he will pick up the kids, he says, and bring them when he comes by to check on me later. However, as the day wears on I am not getting any better.

6p.m. update – WOW!!! My feet hurt!!! Can someone help me? Please help me…anyone!!! I can't stand it; it's like pins and needles shooting through my feet and up my legs. The nurses offer pain medication, and I am insistent that it won't help. I don't like pain medication. I don't take drugs or drink alcohol and haven't for many years. I just want to know what is going on and have someone fix it!!

After a few hours of excruciating pain, I succumb and ask for pain medication. The woman who once was listed as a "difficult patient" during a brief hospital stay for refusing a muscle relaxer is now praying for those darn pain meds. I've given birth to two children, so I'm no stranger to pain, but this was craziness.

By the time Dale, Jessica, and Jonathan come to visit, the pain meds have started to take effect so I am not so uncomfortable. I say not to worry, I will be home probably tomorrow. Jessica wants to stay with me. She is in first grade. She is so sweet, and I hate to see the worry on her small face. Jonathan is too young to understand much, thank God. Dale of course is calm. Yet I can see the concern on his face.

Before I know it, I have to leave them to go for more tests – an MRI, I think. I start to vomit again. The nurses quickly clean me up and off we go. I am so sad for my daughter.

I am sure I have a slipped disk, or so I am trying to convince myself. My gut feeling, though, is that I have MS. Beginning to get frightened.

January 4, 2001

I am worried about work – and increasingly worried and frustrated about what is happening with me physically. Both the CT scan and MRI are negative, thank God, but I am still in a lot of pain.

My mom, my stronghold, is out in the Pacific on a cruise. I can't bother her. What purpose would it serve, except to make her frantic?

Dale and I will just have to wait, and try to cope.

January 5, 2001

I have been assigned a specialist, Dr. Wolfe, who comes to the hospital. When Dr. Wolfe comes in to see me today, I think I must have been introduced to him before but right now I really don't remember. He is young, my age perhaps, and good-looking too.

He sits on my bed – or maybe stands very close, I'm not quite sure – and says, "Erika, we think we know what you have." I feel a burst of relief that ends abruptly with his next words: "You probably won't die but you are going to be sick for a very, very long time."

I stare at him, terrified. Is this MS? Multiple sclerosis is my greatest fear. Dale's father had MS and his grandfather had ALS, so I know what those diseases do to people. I blurt out my concerns and the handsome young doctor, says, "No Erika, it is not MS. It is Guillain-Barre Syndrome. The coating of myelin that surrounds your nerves is being attacked by your own immune system…" He pauses a bit to let me take this in. "Slowly, you will lose movement, and perhaps eventually you will lose all movement and may need to be placed on a ventilator as your lungs are muscles too and may stop working as well. But you will get better."

I lean back, wondering what he means by "sick for a long time." A month? I can handle that – after all, I know, and so does everyone else, that I probably do need some rest and relaxation. I'll deal with this.

Finally, he concludes with, "We will do a spinal tap to confirm that this is what you have." Then he leaves the room and I am alone again.

(*This is long before the days of smartphones, so I cannot just google the disease or ask Siri about it.)

Nighttime

Dale comes to be with me when I get the spinal tap. He is joking and making small talk. This is a welcome relief.

My neurologist, Dr. Commador, is an older gentleman *(*He was probably only in his fifties, which seemed "older" at the time)*. When he comes to get me for the test, he reveals that he'd had Guillain-Barre Syndrome (GBS) less than a year ago – a mild case, he says. Immediately, my mind takes that to mean that I will probably be fine and working within a few months. After all, I am not the sickly type. I will be fine, I tell myself, even though each day it is getting harder to focus and I can't see very well anymore.

Dale stands by my side while he does the spinal tap. The room is cold and sterile. It doesn't really hurt, but I am glad when it's over. I am very tired; I hurt and just want to go to sleep.

January 6th , 2001

"It is confirmed, Erika," Dr. Wolfe says, "You have Guillain-Barre Syndrome." *Should I be relieved?* I am definitely not relieved when they tell me they're moving me down to PCU, the Progressive Care Unit, which is one step above ICU. They explain that this is precautionary, in anticipation of my worsening symptoms. By now I am getting weaker each day. I am finding it hard to even hold my hairbrush.

They explain once again that I may get to the point where I cannot breathe on my own, adding "We hope not, Erika, but just in case." They also assure me that I "will feel more comfortable there."

I am thinking all the while I will *not* feel more comfortable there and am *never* going on a ventilator!!! When they wheel me down to the PCU, all the nurses welcome me like it is a party. *This may be okay,* I think. I hadn't been too happy with the staff on the normal floor so maybe I will see some improvement here. They are all smiling and showing concern as I arrive, which in some strange way makes me feel safer.

My friend John shows up. I don't know him well and it feels awkward. I am hunting for things to say. I look like hell which I would normally be mortified about, but I am getting too sick to care. John tells me all sorts of stupid jokes. He is trying and I am trying to be somewhat alert and charming but failing miserably. I feel like I am starting to die.

I don't remember John leaving. I do remember my kids coming in and wanting to look okay for them but also hoping their visit is short because I am in so much pain. I love my kids so much and I don't want to give them any reason to be worried.

(Friends would tell me later that they came in to see me but I have no recollection. As mentioned, I was getting weaker by the day. I recall the increasing weakness in my limbs and being happy I could still do most of my makeup, though the darn mascara was getting so heavy. As it gets increasingly harder to do these daily activities of living, I await the day when I will not be able to hold the mascara at all. Would I become totally paralyzed, or would it stop before that? I worried every day, "What will tomorrow be like?")

Jan 7, 2001

My mom will be returning to Florida tomorrow. I must tell Dale that we should call her as early as possible before she drives two hours to Sebring, only to have to turn around and drive the one hundred and fifty miles back to Orlando. Secretly I have wanted to call her so badly that I can barely wait any longer. Furthermore, there is the increasing issue of my physical decline – what condition will I be in a few days from now?

I have no idea how Dale and I manage to locate Mom's itinerary and track her down at my stepsister Kathleen's house, but we do.

Now we have a bigger problem: I can barely talk and certainly cannot hold the phone. Mom last saw me over Christmas (Mom had stopped coming for Christmas morning presents, though, as I tended to overindulge and she thought I was spoiling my kids. She was right, too. I loved spoiling my kids!) I know she will be shocked by my condition, and I am sorry to do this to her.

Dale helps me with the phone, and I start talking but get way too tired. Dale finishes the phone call, trying to explain the diagnosis. She is with my stepfather Ron, and they are both very confused. Mostly, I'm so grateful Dale has the ability to hold the phone.

I am so worried that Mom will be nervous, as she has always been a slightly anxious person and it will not take much to send her into a tailspin. But I let go of that worry as I am simply too tired and weak. I thank God for Dale and the nurses. I can't do anything else.

Jan 8, 2001

Mom comes!

Mom and Ron arrive, though I don't recall seeing them walk in. I'm not recalling much as I am sure I am on a lot of pain medication; however, I do remember seeing Ron start to cry.

Ron and Dale leave to give me some alone time with Mom. (Ron has never thought much of my husband, I wonder what he thinks of Dale at this moment as he watches him being so helpful and supportive).

I am alone with Mom and so grateful to have her here with me!! I tell her about my will under the bed. I had made it up a couple of years earlier – an odd thing for a young woman to do but I wanted my kids to know how much I loved them should anything ever happen to me.

I remember feeling stronger just having her there. She asks me about calling my sister Katrina who at the time had been ignoring me for three years. My response is, "Why bother – she didn't talk to me when I was well so why reach out now that I am sick!" I've always wished my sister and I were closer, but this is definitely not the time to repair relationships.

Later in the evening:

The nurse, a lovely older lady (*She is also in her fifties, and as it's taken me twenty years to write this it no longer sounds so old!*), comes in. She is concerned with my breathing. I am more irritated that my time with Mom has been interrupted. The nurse is now pounding on my back, and it reminds me of the medical staff doing this to my son when he was a baby and had breathing difficulties due to asthma, RSV, and a host of other problems he thankfully outgrew.

She explains that this will loosen the phlegm and aid in breathing. I know all this already, but I let her talk. She apologizes for hitting me so hard and says, "Perhaps this will keep you off the breathing machine another night." I am thinking to myself, *Lady, you are crazy! I am NOT going on a breathing machine!*

When the nurse is done, Mom and I talk about fear and death and love and life. I remember saying (and this is profound and true), "You worry your whole life about six things and it is the seventh one that gets you." Worry is useless.

My profound statement is of little comfort when the doctor walks in and announces that I am going to the ICU that night in preparation for respiratory failure.

I am irritated!! I am not going into respiratory failure, and, furthermore, I need to have my hair washed. I usually wash it every day, and now it is a dirty mess. I start to cry.

(*Today, as a mental health counselor I would think this was some sort of denial or aversion, but I was really concerned about my hair! I had always washed it every day, and it was now so dirty that it was driving me crazy.)

God love them, the nurse (and, gosh, I wish I could recall her name to give her credit) and my mother wash my hair!! I am almost totally paralyzed, and they figure out a way to make this work.

It's about 4 a.m., my hair is washed, and I am off to the ICU. I am anxious about what the ICU is like; obviously, I have never been there before.

January 9, 2001

I arrive in the ICU. My nurse is Dan (*a man I will grow to love). He is a nice-looking man probably about my age. He is polite and very thorough. He says people will be checking on me all the time. I want to talk but he is busy. Mom leaves to go home and get some sleep. They won't let her spend but ten minutes every hour with me; that is the rule here.

I finally go to sleep, feeling safe and somewhat pleased that at least my hair is clean.

(*I must say that NEVER did I feel victimized. Never did I question, why me? In fact, I felt very grateful that if someone was going to get some odd, rare, horrendous syndrome it was me. I somehow knew I could handle it. I could take the pain.)

Later same day

Dale comes in to visit. I am glad to see him. We talk like old friends over coffee. The neurologist calls in and says my numbers aren't so good. He wants to put me on a ventilator immediately to avoid an emergency later. I am furious. I don't want this and say so, but it doesn't matter; it is going to happen. As everyone begins to rush around, I am suddenly terrified. *Please God, help me*, I cry, *What is happening to me?*

I am totally aware of everything going on around me.

As it is nighttime, Dan is back, thank goodness, but they say Dale must leave for the procedure (*yes, being put on a ventilator is a "procedure". I could have certainly used his calming presence during this experience, but it is not in the cards.)

They are having trouble inserting the ventilator. I'm thinking, *Why is this taking so long? Why isn't it going smoothly?* It is terribly uncomfortable as well. *Please leave me alone.*

Finally, the ventilator is in; however, no one has instructed me on how it works. Do I breathe with it, or hold my breath? Of course, I can't ask as I have a tube in my mouth. I am furious with myself for not having asked before they did this!

Dale is back, thank God, and he is crying and looking concerned. Inside I am screaming, "Please don't leave me" and somehow, he understands. He says he will stay for his ten minutes every hour and as it is around midnight we both have long nights ahead of us.

Jan 11, 2001

Mom comes to visit. I am told I start to cry. I can't talk with this ventilator in my mouth. I don't remember being agitated but I am later told that this is when I tried to bite a nurse, so I guess I was.

I am told I am going to receive Rohypnol (or Dipnoan), a drug to make me forget what is happening…it works. *(*I do have lucid moments and memories, though even those are sketchy at best. Thankfully, my mother thought to put together an outline of events so we would have a record.)*

Jan 13, 2001

Dale is friendly with all the nurses. He is very people-smart and knows treating them well will result in my being looked after better.

Dale is also very friendly with the other folks in the ICU waiting room. He meets someone who had Guillain-Barre Syndrome. He asks if I'd like to meet him and I nod yes; I mean, obviously I'm looking for any sign of hope!

I meet the man. He is there because his daughter is sick and very concerned for her. He tells me that Guillain-Barre is rough, scary, and frustrating BUT I will live. This will get better. And then he is off. Gone, no more hope, no more explanation.

I can't imagine that he lived through this. Well, clearly, he is alive, but was his condition as serious as mine? Is he lying? Was he on a ventilator?

I am so frustrated. I go to a spot of surrender in my mind. I decide to just lie there and hope this all goes away.

At least Dale is here, I always feel better when he is here. I think some way, someday this will all be over.

Jan ?, 2001

Nightmares!! The scariest of nightmares. My recollections are fuzzy. I am fighting everything and everyone. I can't communicate with anyone. I don't know if anyone even tries to talk with me. I keep biting the ventilator to get it out of my mouth *(*and apparently biting staff, including a wonderful nurse named Gina),* so they place a mask over my face to keep me from doing so. I start slamming my head from side to side. This is because I can only move my head and I am showing my utter frustration. Even one eye is paralyzed. *(*I am so happy I don't remember this part. I was told this by my mother and Dale. They said they had never seen anyone fight so hard. They even had to use duct tape to wrap the mask in place so I didn't get it off. The duct tape does nothing for my long blonde hair, but that story is for another day .)*

Jan 23, 2001

Today is my dear darling daughter's seventh birthday. When they first diagnosed me, I had been so worried about not being home for it. I told Jessica we would have a big party for her when I got out. I knew this wouldn't solve a thing, but it was an attempt. She was my firstborn. It had been just her and I for the first three years of her life – *how could I not be there for her birthday?!* But it was happening, whether I liked it or not. *(*By this date I was unaware of my daughter, or anything else. I was in and out of a medically-induced coma; to alleviate some of the suffering, both physical and mental. Days slipped by like sand. The only constant was the pain and fear.)*

Jan 24, 2001

I am given a swallow study to determine if I can ingest food or liquid on my own. *(I do not recall the test; I was told later that not only did I fail, I PROFOUNDLY failed. Looking back, I wonder why they thought a woman who could not breathe on her own would be able to swallow! I also learned that they want to insert a permanent feeding tube in my stomach. What do I care? I feel as if I have lost my life at this point anyway.*

My mother almost decided not to give me one as she felt I was not going to recover. While sequestered in the bathroom so the kids would not hear her, she had a phone *call* with the doctor, He *talked her into it. I chose my mother as my medical proxy as Dale was busy working during the day and Mom came to the hospital during rounding hours. I had thought Mom ran most decisions by Dale but that didn't always happen. Dale would not have hesitated to give me a feeding tube. We all handle things differently. Dale wouldn't have given up on me, ever. Mom, I'm sure was nervous I'd be a "vegetable," dependent on machines to keep me alive.)*

Jan 25, 2001

Today is my dear mother's birthday. How I wish I knew what day it was. I am just fighting for my life.

Jan 26, 2001

I have been transferred from ORMC to its sister hospital, Lucerne Hospital (*which no longer exists*). I think it's more like the *ugly stepsister* hospital. It is where you are sent when you are making no progress. At this moment, I am unaware of my health status, only that I have essentially lost my life.

*(*I had been to Lucerne once before when my son Jonathan was really sick with the croup and an asthma attack. We spent the entire*

night in the ER because they didn't know if they should admit him or not. Once they decided not to admit him, I raced back home to put on work clothes and get to the office. This was my pace. Now I am not going anywhere.)

I lay there in the new room. The sun seems very bright, like I have come to after a long slumber. I am starting to recall things. By this time, I have had a tracheotomy, which is a hole in my trachea so a more permanent apparatus for artificial breathing can keep me alive. It is more comfortable than having the tube in my mouth and they usually perform this procedure for those who have been on a ventilator for a while. It also gives me another advantage: although I cannot speak, I can mouth words for anyone willing to try to make sense of them.

Some of my first thoughts are: *Why is it so hot in here? Please pull more covers off me or something.* I've never been a hot person. I was always cold but now this has changed in a big way. *(*No one can understand it until months later, when we find out that GBS affects the "temperature control center" located at the top of the spinal cord.)*

I see Mom amidst the doctors and nurses. I see Ron too. President Bush is on the TV, but I just brush over this *(*which is notable because I had voted for him during what turned out to be a long, tense election process that centered largely on Florida and was especially difficult for its residents. I normally would have been very interested in watching the inauguration.)*

I ask Mom repeatedly to please, please take me home. She says she can't. I feel so lost, alone, frustrated. Just crushed. Please someone help me!

Jan 27, 2001

Praise God, someone has put a huge fan in my room. I can breathe, not literally (obviously), but at least now I am cooler.

I am having many nightmares. Maybe they are hallucinations, but boy they seem real. It's like someone is taking me all over the hospital at nighttime when my family is not around.

Jan 28, 2001

Questions arise about my children. I don't want them to see me like this. They will be scared. Moreover, I felt like the dependent child. How could I possibly help them?

I don't feel like the nurses are taking good care of me (*and, for the most part, I was right!) They seem hurried and impatient, especially when they move me. (*I don't know if they thought that because I was paralyzed I had no sensory feeling, but this was not true. To clean me they moved me quickly and it was so painful.) I want to tell them to stop and that they were hurting me, but I am unable to say a word. I began to cry inside every time I saw the nurse's aides coming to bathe me. I wanted so much to communicate but there was no way. None of them even took the time to look me in the eye.

I do have one terrific nurse, Carrie Beth. I feel safe with her. She seems to appear whenever I am just about at the end of my rope, almost as if she's able to intuit my needs as clearly as if I had stated them. (*Or that I was in fact being watched over, that God, Jesus, some greater force was carrying me...)

Carrie Beth's boyfriend works here as well, as a respiratory therapist. I think he lacks personality, though he is very competent. (*In fact, one day, he would save my life. I will go into this later.)

Chapter 4

Hallucinations or Reality?
(Both are Terrifying)

Feb 1, 2001

I am having more hallucinations. I think I am all better – *why are they keeping me here?* Then I think they are trying to keep me sick. I become very paranoid.

My hallucinations become more real to me than reality. I am no longer operating in the real world, but in a haze of drugs penetrated only by an agony I am not able to express.

The pain is most unbearable when they move me. They turn me on my side so they can clean me up *(not all potty issues are resolved by the catheter)*. I would normally have been so embarrassed but at this point I am seeing colors from the pain. They appear like a rainbow in front of my eyes. I want to scream, "Go slow!" I want to say anything, but I have no ability. (*I will go through this every time I go to the bathroom, or they decide to give me a sponge bath, and it will continue for months.*)

Early February

Blackness and more blackness. I remember little else of these early days, due to the Rohypnol they have given me.

(That was preferable in the moment, but later I would wish I could remember. It's as if two months were stolen from me. (Since then, this has served as a reminder of how precious time is). That is a long time to not know what I said (given the tracheotomy I guess it wasn't much) what I did or what happened to me. It's an eerie feeling. Ron told me I'd complain about the pain until I got medication, then I'd stare at the ceiling or walls until it wore off at which point, I'd become agitated again.)

Feb. 2, 2001

For the first time in a long time, I am awake and lucid. It is early and quiet, except for the humming sound coming from my bed (the ventilator). I am confused and startled by my surroundings. I am alone in my room, a hospital room. I can hear someone talking outside the door and guess that it's a nurse and my mother. Please God, let it be my mother. She can help me make sense of this. I try to speak but no words come out. I want so much to move. I think if I just try hard enough, I can push through and at the very least fall off my bed onto the hospital room floor. This proves to be impossible.

I see men walking on the roof outside my window. *How can this be?*

My mother comes into the room. It feels like the first time in weeks I have communicated with her. *"Am I okay?"* I mouth. *"Where am I? I see men walking on the roof out my window, well now I am really scared!! Am I losing my mind?"* Mom laughs a little at the last comment and says "Erika, you are not seeing things. There *are* men walking on the roof doing construction!" I am quite relieved and happy to be conscious and able to communicate, even if it's silently. Mom tells me what has been happening with me over the last few weeks. *I keep losing time. I don't like this!*

Feb. 3, 2001

I have a nurse from the "pool" today. These are nurses that fill in and float wherever they are needed in the hospital. Floaters are usually not my favorites. They don't know what is going on with me or my care. They also know that they will probably never run into me again and they may have an entirely different background than what is necessary for my case. However, today I have a wonderful floater. She is warm and friendly and, best of all, she comes from New Jersey!

I felt very safe with her, making it a good day for me. I vividly remember her asking me to come see her house *(This is one of the hallucinations that sticks with me twenty years later. Dale was part of that hallucination as I thought he came to her house as well and we were laying on her floor with a bunch of blankets — whew! I thought this for a very long time and even out of the ICU it was hard to convince me otherwise. After a patient is admitted for a long time, they lose sense of time. Drugs and pain only complicate the matter. This is called hospital psychosis, and it is real.* Most of the time, I believe that I am still living in New Jersey, specifically our beautiful home in Bernardsville, where we were living when we got married. That was one of my favorite times in my life so I guess it's not surprising that I mentally traveled back there. Dale told people not to argue with me and let me believe we were still there.)

Feb. 4, 2001

I am lying in bed as usual but now I am about to have plasmapheresis. *(Plasmapheresis, also known as plasma exchange, is a procedure that removes harmful antibodies from the blood and is useful in treating autoimmune conditions)* I have had this done many times before, but this is the first time I remember it. They stick a tube in my neck, which sort of scares me. I believe I also have another needle in my chest. Then they tell me to relax – hmmm. I want to ask questions, but that's not happening. At least it doesn't hurt.

It seems to take sooo long. Mom is with me. I remember the sun shining in on us; it calms me. The sun always calms me. I wish I was outside, living. At least my favorite nurse is on today, she comes in with another nurse and asks if I need anything. Mom says no, and they leave for lunch. They mention they are walking to the restaurant, and I can actually smell the fragrant spring air and feel the sun on my shoulders. I want so much to go with them – if only I could get out of the hospital bed. I try again to move, but of course, it is futile.

Somewhere inside of me, I know I will be better. I know that although it doesn't look good at the moment and many doctors and medical staff are giving up on me. I know I will get out of this bed and walk in the springtime air once again. I am determined. I have way too many wonderful things to live for. I have children that need me. I cannot quit.

(*Indeed, I was far sicker than most thought I would become, and I was getting worse. Both plasmapheresis and IVIG (or intravenous immunoglobulin, where they give the patient the albumin, a protein made by the liver, of a healthy person) have failed miserably. I kept getting pneumonia from lying on my back and being on a ventilator. The chest tubes being used to drain the fluid from my

lungs were not adequate. I was clinging to life and the pain was still
unbearable. But I was determined.)

Feb. 5, 2001

I am fitted with a Passy Muir valve, a valve that can be inserted
when someone has a trach and allows them to speak (it puts air
on the vocal cords). I'm thrilled to finally be able to talk, though
each time I want to do so the respiratory therapist has to come
in and lower the cuff on the valve. There is a lot of phlegm and
mucus involved in clearing the airway so having the cuff lowered
is never pleasant. (From what I've been told, I said some pretty
off the wall things when this was happening. One day, I made the
nurses take the cuff down, so I could talk to the doctor. Everyone
waited patiently for me to utter a sentence, this after the trach
had been suctioned and a lot of choking, only to hear me say "I
think I'd like to have another baby.")

Still, I am so grateful to finally be able to talk to Mom. I have
wanted so much to tell her of all the atrocities that take place
in the hospital, and now I can! I tell her about my least favorite
nurse's aide who comes barging into my room every morning
and sticks the thermometer under my arm and never even looks
at me. On the rare occasion when she does look at me, she just
talks at me, never stopping to see my reaction or to read my
lips. I tell Mom I'm scared. I have no way to call for help. I
can't exactly press a call bell. And this has been true for many
weeks now.

Next, I ask Mom if she thinks I am going to die. She answers
honestly. She is very worried that I won't make it through this. I
know I am very sick, but I had never realized until this moment
that even my family might be giving up on me. I am strong-
willed. I know I can pull through just about anything – at least,

that had been true prior to this crazy illness. I had been through many hard times, but nothing had ever held me down for long. Now my body was failing me, which was completely uncharted territory – but I would forge on…

Using this Passy Muir valve is so uncomfortable that I ultimately go back to mouthing words. This is very problematic, as many don't understand what I am trying to say, and most don't take the time to try. (It must have been very frustrating for all, but I was so over it! I couldn't get simple requests right, and I remember them using a board of pictures they would point at, then I would bat my eyes two times for yes and once for no. What I wanted usually wasn't on the board, go figure. Also, the eye that was paralyzed remained frozen in the open position, and they had to tape it shut so I could sleep and so it would not get too dried out. *What if the other eye got paralyzed?)*

Feb. 6, 2001

Mom walks in to see me. It is always so good to see her. I don't feel alone or frightened when she comes. I feel the same way when Dale comes in the evenings. I don't think I would have survived had it not been for them.

Mom says she has a surprise for me. I can't imagine what it is and furthermore, I can't think of any sort of surprise that might make me happy. Mom tells me she has a tape from my little Jessica! I am thrilled and sad (I miss her so much). I also feel so guilty for not being home with her and Jonathan, so many feelings at the same time. But through all my mixed emotions, joy takes center stage as I hear her little sweet voice on the recorder. She still loves me and misses me, and she sounds okay, amazingly she sounds okay. God has given me such a gift in her. I am at a loss as to how to help her and yet there she is helping me.

I immediately want to tape a message back to her. I don't even feel self-conscious about my breathy voice, (I assume they used the Passy Muir valve to aid in my communication), and I do not have to think for two seconds about what to say to her. It simply flows out of me for my angel child. God how I wish I could hug her and hold her, but I am in no way ready for this yet. I am still afraid to have them see me like this plus I have staph infections that make it too dangerous.

Feb. 7, 2001

At this point I am so foggy I can't tell one day from the next *(in fact according to Mom's notes the following occurred two days prior)* however, this morning sticks out in my mind like few others. It is the morning I didn't think I would make it.

I had lain awake in the stillness of the night. This wasn't unusual for me; I awoke a lot due to the hospital setting. Also, days and nights blended together like a never-ending nightmare. I remember being disoriented and couldn't tell if I had been sleeping, hallucinating, or a combination of both. I started having heaviness in my chest, then it moved up to my throat. I felt like I couldn't breathe. *Oh no*, I silently screamed, *I can't breathe! HELP, dear God, someone help me.* I banged my head on the souped-up call bell they had finally made me; unfortunately, it would later fail and they would have to find another way for me to call for help. I thank God this had been set up. The nurse finally comes in, but I can't talk to tell her I can't breathe. I think I am going to die now. I see a blue light off in the distance (I don't know what the blue signifies but I know I am not getting oxygen). Perhaps it signifies death? Although I remember thinking it was strange that it was blue – *Only I would see a blue light guiding me to the other side!* My nurse is fumbling around. She is trying to adjust things on the ventilator, but nothing is working.

Luckily the respiratory therapist (and the boyfriend of my favorite nurse, Cary Beth) isn't far away and rushes in. He has an Ambu bag (manual resuscitator) and, uttering harsh words, pushes the nurse aside and pushes the Ambu bag on my mouth, forcing air into my lungs. He can remove the mucus clot that has restricted my breathing. (I am sure he had to suction my lungs, but I only recall the Ambu bag, and him shouting at the nurse, "You could have killed her!")

My life has been spared again, but now I am even more terrified of the inept nurses and most of the time they are all I have.

Feb. 8 & 9, 2001

My Aunt Priscilla came to visit with my cousin Adrienne. (*I want to say I remember this, but it is a blur, and I can't tell if I am now remembering some of it because I have been told about it.*)

My family rallied around me during these early days. Cousins I had lost contact with sent flowers, balloons, and cards. Thanksgiving of the previous year we'd had a beautiful family reunion. It was wonderful. I had not seen some – actually, most – of my extended family for years. Now, I thanked God for those memories, which were so comforting as I lay there on death's door. I thought to myself many times, as I lay there looking at the Coke machine outside my door, that memories are all you really have in the end. Memories of cherished family and times, so sweet and fleeting.

My being sick changed my thinking completely. I had a complete change in perception. Not that I didn't have an appreciation of family and life before I got sick, I certainly did, but it really got cemented in my mind while I was paralyzed in bed. I realized the *only* thing that truly mattered to me was family, dear friends, and spiritual beliefs.

Feb. 10, 2001

My cousins send me a Vermont Teddy Bear. I am incredibly touched and wishing I could touch it. They also send balloons. I muster up the strength to tell Mom they should go home to Jonathan. He loves balloons and will have a great time with them. My sweet angel – it had been so long since I had seen him or my other angel, Jessica.

Along with the ache for my children is the guilt for not being home with them. I feel like a failure for getting sick *(a feeling that will persist long after getting well)*. I feel like a failure that I'm not home, at my job, or even mopping my floors. I had always *been such a neat freak I used to mop every night. So much was out of my control but not being there for my children horrified me the most.)*

Tomorrow, my kids are scheduled to come see me for the first time in six weeks. I am so worried. What will they think? Will they be frightened of all the tubes attached to me and coming out of every orifice of my body? What will they think of the ventilator? And my God, my hair and my face with no makeup!! My hair has been washed once in those six weeks. I asked my dear friend Cathy to come do my makeup before my kids arrive and she lovingly agrees. I am so excited, yet terrified to see them. They are very young, seven and two, I wonder if they have a sense of the same feeling.

Feb. 11, 2001

I wake very early in the morning and am unable to go back to sleep. I am nervous that Cathy won't get to put my makeup on in time, so at 5:30 a.m. I ask the night nurse to do it. She obliges, and I don't know how she understands my request, let alone finds the time to do it. I am certain she thinks I am half-crazy.

So now I am all made up dozing in and out. I hallucinate that I am lying in something like an army hospital. I am afraid of not being able to breathe again when my dear Cathy pops in and greets me. My wonderful friend, she has remembered and is here in plenty of time. She is very surprised to see me all made up already! She talks to me and calms me down for hours before the big visit.

Late morning:

Mom is here. I think she comes before everybody. I want to wear a certain nightgown. Mom is trying to explain to me that it will never get over my head with all the tubes and ventilator attached. Mom decides it is good enough to just lay the gown on top of me. I am furious. Why can't she get it on? My heart rate soars. The nurses and mom are now threatening to cancel the visit.

Still, I remain adamant about wearing this blue nightgown. Another lovely nurse comes in with a blue tie to use as an ascot around my throat to cover the trach. Lord knows I had tubes everywhere and I understand now why they couldn't comply with my demands, but at the time all I could think of was how I needed to appear as normal as possible for my children.

As I calm down, I allow the ascot to be put on with the nightgown draped over me. I feel now as ready as I'll ever be to see Jessica and Jonathan.

Unbeknown to me, my mother has worked with Jessica prior to her coming to prepare her for my appearance. Jessica even drew a picture of what she thought I would look like. I saw it later, and she was pretty spot-on. Mom was thoughtful that way. Jessica is so loving that she probably would have just accepted me anyhow, but I wanted her to have faith that I was going to be okay.

At first, when Jessica comes in with Mom and Ron, she is a bit apprehensive. Still, she smiles and runs to my side amidst all the tubes and machines. There is so much I want to say but, I can only cry. She cries too. So, there we are, crying together with her hugging me. All I can seem to spit out (via my Passy Muir valve) is how much I've missed her. I also say that these are happy tears that keep falling from my eyes, *but this is not true. They are a mixture of happy, sad, guilty…the list could go on.)*

Now Dale enters with Jonathan in his arms. My son is small and beautiful, just as I remember him, my baby boy. But he is not smiling. He is frightened and starts to cry. Dale tries to put him on my bed; he sits for a few moments and then gets nervous. He goes back to Daddy and says, "Mommy has a boo-boo." My heart breaks for him; he is so young to have to see his mommy like this. When I was well, I was all he ever wanted. When I left the room, he would cry. He lived on my left hip most of the time. Dale used to joke that women have an extra bone in their hips to carry their children.

Jessica just stays hugging me, crying with me. I wish I could smile and say it all would be alright, but those words will not come out. It's not alright, not even close. In six short weeks, our worlds had all been turned upside down.

Feb. 13, 2001

I have somehow made a wonderful friend, a male nurse whose name now escapes me. He is not my usual nurse, and I can't talk, so how this friendship formed is a complete mystery. I suppose people feel sorry for me and befriend me out of the goodness of their hearts. Whatever the case, he comes to visit me periodically and tells me about his son.

I am so grateful he came to visit me this morning. I had awoken feeling tremendous heaviness in my chest. My breathing felt very shallow and difficult to perform. I felt frightened and tried to tell my nurse. She didn't believe me. She checked my ventilator connection and told me I was fine. Not much else I could do but lay there.

I didn't really begin to panic until the respiratory therapist also declared me "fine." inside myself I was screaming, *I can't breathe!*, then I started mouthing the words (I had all but sworn off the Passy Muir valve – I hated that damn thing), but no one paid attention. I lay there alone and frightened, thinking for sure I would die before anyone believed me. Thankfully, my new friend came in and asked me how I was doing. I somehow informed him that I could not breathe very well, and he immediately took action. He got my regular nurse's attention and told her to call a doctor. Before I knew it, I was being wheeled into X-Ray, and they found my left lung filled with fluid. It is called a pneumothorax (a partially collapsed lung), caused by air and blood creating a pocket. In fact, I was drowning and could feel it.

They told me they had to do minor surgery to insert a drainage tube into my lung. All I could think was, *HURRY UP, I'M DYING HERE.* They inserted the tube, relieving the blood and fluid.

I now have a huge drum next to my bed into which my lung drains…but I'm still alive, still hanging in there somehow. Perhaps it was God intervening.

Feb. 14, 2001

My dear friend from work, Jackie, comes to visit. She has a big card signed by just about everyone I worked with at Darden Corporate Headquarters. I am deeply moved by the gesture, as well as by Jackie, who comes by often. The first time she came my mother was worried about how she would respond to seeing me in the ICU, hooked up to so many tubes and machines. Jackie just pushed past all of it and embraced me. I am so lucky to be so loved.

Back when things were normal, Jackie and I used to talk for hours about our husbands and how crazy they made us, or about our beautiful children. Boy, I would have given the world to be having one of those conversations now, and I know Jackie would too.

Dale arrives later with his own card (he brings a card every day) along with lovely emerald earrings for Valentine's Day. He wanted to put them in for me, but at this time I am particularly confused and not caring much about Valentine's Day. Furthermore, I did not want to be touched. I was tired and in pain; however, Dale's presence reminded me that I was loved; it was the greatest gift I could have received. Dale just sat with me and left the earrings for another day. Believe me, for my husband to buy me earrings was a huge deal – not because he didn't have the heart, but because he didn't have the money.

Money, although necessary, means so little…it means absolutely nothing when one is on a ventilator in a lot of pain.

Feb. 15, 2001

Dale comes for his usual evening visit. I love it when he comes and am usually growing pretty impatient by the time he arrives around 8:00 p.m. Mom, who is with me most of the day, leaves by 4:30 p.m. at the latest to get the kids from daycare and school.

Those three and a half hours I am by myself seem like an eternity. I sleep, watch TV, and sleep some more. Sometimes there is hospital business to take care of such as X-Rays, suctioning of my trach, or other unpleasant "to-dos."

Tonight, I have a surprise for Dale, the nurse has put my new earrings in! He is thrilled that I like them. I am hardly the wife he is used to, practically a shadow of the "double-A" personality he used to joke about, but I am wearing the earrings and he knows I am happy he got them. For that moment, it is enough.

Feb. 16, 2001

Today, I have a new visitor, Norma Stanley, the attorney my mom has retained to create a will and trust for me. Mom has been very concerned about our family's finances. She is worried that if I die all my savings will go to the IRS as Dale owes them quite a bit of money, a debt he incurred prior to our marriage. Not knowing the legalities, Mom's mind races to my death, all the money being then in Dale's name and the IRS doing a money grab that would negatively affect Jessica and Jonathan's quality of life. She also knows that I have been the breadwinner and took great care to provide for our family. She wants to make sure my children will not go without.

I do have the will I wrote a couple of years ago. It wasn't something I planned; I wasn't even thirty-six at the time and had never given it much thought before. But one night when the kids were sleeping and Dale was still back in New Jersey, the thought suddenly hit me: *What if something happens to me?* I wrote it all out, but I never had it notarized. Mom was able to find it but remains concerned that because it is not notarized it will not hold up in court. She does some investigating and decides it is probably best for me to create a trust.

Finances are the last thing on my mind. My head starts spinning at just the mention of the subject, but, too weak to fight and too drugged to think, I agree. Maybe a trust would be best – what do I know at this point? (I wish my husband was more involved in this decision. Yes, protecting my assets was important to the kids, but he did so much for me and I didn't want him to be excluded in any way.)

As I write this journal, I am very aware that money is nothing. There is not enough money in the world to have someone sit vigil by your bedside every night. Lucky was I to have this support. Many folks do not have family or friends to support them. These situations can happen to anyone – no one is exempt. Life is not fair and it is no one's fault.

Anyway, today I am to sign the trust papers. Norma tries to make conversation, saying how she "feels" for me and my family at this time. I am annoyed and very curt with her. I am angry. I feel antagonized and patronized by her and her stupid small talk. How can she possibly have any idea of what this is like? I do not need her pity, nor do I like her fake sympathy. I also find myself feeling even more distrustful (it's not like I can even read what I am signing! Also, bear in mind that when I say I am literally mouthing words and feel lucky when people make an attempt to guess at them, let alone get the communication correctly. In fact, I am lucky when people even attempt to see that I am trying to communicate and am coherent.). All I want is for this meeting to come to a close. Finally, I tell Norma to leave the papers and I will sign them later (*My arrogance is almost funny to me as I write this as just how was this going to happen, really? I can't see well, I am drugged, and I can't hold a pen.)

In retrospect, I think I just felt so out of control. Someone else is doing my finances, making my decisions. Telling Norma to leave the papers gives me a small sense of control and I feel more at ease.

Later, I did manage to sign the papers (with the help of someone, who held my hand so I could make an X, or something like it), though I didn't review them until I got out of the hospital. I *also* insisted, though, that all my family be taken care of, *including* Dale. I knew this was not what Mom wanted, but I wanted it. I didn't care that he had been financially irresponsible; he loved me and helped me, and neither money nor love work that way.

Chapter 5

Everybody Needs a Break

Feb. 17, 2001

*M*om is going to take Jessica back to her home in Sebring for a few days. I know I should be happy, but I feel abandoned and alone. Hell, I *am* alone. I can't imagine how I will get by the next few days without her. I remember thinking when Mom told me she needed a break and so did Jessica, that I could have used one as well!

Then I remember that Mom and Ron had come straight from their cruise to the hospital. Their lives had been upended as well. Ron has since gone home, and Mom surely wants to see him and sleep in her own bed for a while. I know caretakers certainly need breaks, but what about the people in the bed? They remain sick. They remain in the bed and there are no breaks for them. Yes, sometimes things become too difficult for caretakers to handle, but ignoring those things or walking out the door doesn't mean the problem goes away.

(This is the mental health counselor coming out in me. Who is there for the sick? Many times, no one. Those who are strongly

supported always do better. I had a lot of support from family and friends. I know this is why I am alive today.)

Going home. It's a luxury I can't even imagine right now. Breathing on my own would be a luxury. I start bargaining in my head saying things like, "I wouldn't even mind if I wasn't able to walk. Just to be able to breathe on my own would be enough."

Mom's trip is not the only thing on my mind today. I'm worried about work and the fact that I left Lisa, my boss, stranded. I was able to have Ron write a letter to her before they left. I really like and respect Lisa, and am genuinely concerned about what is going on at Darden while I am lying paralyzed on a vent.

More importantly, I am once again having breathing difficulties. This happens sometimes, however, today it is particularly bad. Mom tells me my stats are fine and not to worry, but I feel like I can't breathe. The alarm goes off for the ventilator and the respiratory therapist comes in with the Ambu bag which pushes oxygen into my lungs until they can fix the issue, I don't know what the issue is, but I am grateful to God for saving my life once again.

Feb. 18, 2001

With Mom gone, the days pass like molasses going uphill. My heart is ripped out that I am not the one taking my little Jessica away for a few days; that is normally my job.

I know I can't worry about Mom's departure or my kids for too long. Basic breathing is challenging. The pain is excruciating. So, it's about priorities. But with Mom gone, the days are very long.

Feb. 22, 2001

Mom is back. I am much more relaxed. But now I want to go home – desperately, I want to go home. I beg Mom as she leaves for the day, but she says she can't take me. I tell her they can just put me upstairs in my home with the ventilator. Mom tries to explain that that won't work.

I am experiencing more complications. The chest tube won't get rid of all the fluid around the lung. They are now saying I need to have full-on lung surgery; however, they are also stating that I am not yet strong enough for it. This doesn't sound so good to me, and I begin to get concerned, more accurately, I am getting *more* concerned. I don't want to take any more pain medication. It is making me too out of it. I need to think clearly with all that is going on (not to mention the terrible ongoing hallucinations caused by the meds and the long hospitalization).

Feb. 23, 2001

More fluid is forming outside the lung and keeps it from expanding. Surgery will have to be performed to scrape the lung and despite my weakened condition it must be done imminently. I may even need a lobectomy or a partial removal of the lung. There is much talk about whether I will survive the surgery, but without it I will probably never get off the ventilator.

This is when my stepfather steps up and says to my very nervous mother and doctors, "You have no choice. She would rather die than not get better and potentially live on a ventilator the rest of her life." Ron knows my spirit and is not afraid to say it like it is, clearly and directly. I have always thanked him for that. It is indeed my only option to ever get off the ventilator or even have a chance to live. So, all in, let's go. There is one more hurdle, however, I am very sick. I feel very nauseous. They say I have some sort of flu or a bug. I have no idea; I just know I am totally paralyzed and now sick as hell to my stomach. I feel like I am dying. Some days I want to die. But again, no one is paying attention to my nausea. They claim I am nervous about the surgery; I know this is not the case.

Feb. 24, 2001

My sister Katrina and her daughter Sarah have come in to visit me. I know Sarah must be frightened, she is a couple of years older than my Jessica and seeing all the tubes and hearing the ventilator is hard on most adults. I try to show a brave face for Sarah. I am her auntie, after all, and the little girl knows nothing of the bad blood between her mother and myself. I can't move and am still so sick. I mouth that I can't talk as I am not feeling well so Sarah doesn't have to stay long and honestly, it is the truth. I feel *sooo* sick.

I am curious as to why my sister is here. She had stopped talking to me about two years ago, and it was always an on-and-off relationship. I believe she was getting divorced and that was when she cut me off, but I didn't understand why. I had asked her to be Jonathan's godmother and she never even responded. Now Jonathan was two and a half and I still had no idea what had happened between us. I try to recall and think that Mom and I tried to call again that past Christmas, just as I was getting sick, but she didn't call back then either. As mentioned in a prior entry, when I had first gotten sick Mom asked if I wanted her to contact Katrina and I simply asked, "Why?" It saddens me to this day that our relationship has been tumultuous. She is my only blood sister, and I am sure she has her own side of the story. (In retrospect, it was very kind of her to come.)

Anyway, she is here now. I think to myself, *This can't be a good sign, I must be pretty bad off,* followed by, *If I felt any better this might be uncomfortable.*

Feb. 25, 2001

Today is the day I am going back to ORMC, the "good hospital," for my lung surgery.

I am still feeling so sick, but no one on the hospital staff seems to care. As mentioned, they tell me that I am just nervous about the procedure. Truly, I am not that nervous about the surgery. It needs to be done. Do it. I have been through so many atrocities that one more hardly scares me.

As they are getting ready to transport me, I ask in my way, "How am I going to breathe on the ride over?" My nurse today is Nora, one of the few I really like, "I am going to ride with you," she says, and then shows me the Ambu bag.

No one explains any further, but I soon get the sense that she is going to use the bag to manually breathe for me the entire ride. I am thinking, *Oh shit, what if she messes this up? This can't be possible – who could do this?* Terrified but with absolutely no choice in the matter, I say a silent prayer that Nora knows what she is doing.

In hospitals, things move very slowly…until they don't. Once they are ready for you, they all move with lightning speed.

I am disconnected from the ventilator and quickly wheeled to the ambulance, then we are off. Nora bags me the entire ride, literally breathing for me. I am amazed. She never looks away. She never stops. It does not stop my terror, but we are doing it.

I arrive at my old stomping grounds, ORMC. I am so grateful to have made it. I am greeted back in the ICU by Dan my favorite and most proficient nurse. As he puts me back on the ventilator, I recall that I was not always so fond of Dan. On occasion his tone and all-around bedside manner appeared to be one of impatience, but that had changed when I realized that I was always in good hands with him. My appreciation of this man has grown abundantly,

One of the most admirable things about Dan is that he is so detail-oriented. I have learned that his demeanor demonstrates how seriously he takes his job. Now, one might think these qualities are the norm for an ICU nurse, but unfortunately that is not the case.

Dan begins to slowly and methodically check me over – my arms, my legs, catheter, trach, feeding tube…and that's when he abruptly stops. He looks at me and asks, with shock and anger in his tone, "What is this?" I am thinking, *How do I know? I can't even see my stomach.* He knows I do not have an answer, and that even if I did I wouldn't be able to vocalize it. As Dan has never been able to read my lips (he has tried on occasion but he's usually thinking ten steps ahead and doesn't have the time to figure out what I'm saying), he runs out to get Dale who is, as always, waiting patiently outside.

Dale enters and Dan pulls up my hospital gown and repeats, "What the hell is this?" Dale looks stunned. "Look at her stomach," Dan says, "It is very distended. What happened?" He then says something about my looking like I'm three months pregnant, which we all know is not true.

Dan checks more things and says, "Your stomach is full of fluid. I think the feeding tube is not working." Finally, someone has figured out why I feel so nauseous!

Dan proceeds to siphon two and a half liters of undigested feeding tube fluid from my stomach. A few tests later, they conclude that there is nothing wrong with the feeding tube – it is my stomach that cannot pass food. I have an ileus, which is basically a temporary slow-down or paralysis of the intestinal muscles.

I am not sure when or how my sister Katrina enters the picture, but suddenly she is there with Dale and Dan. Katrina is not one to hold back and if you want your case heard, she is your woman.

I have already vomited a few times and although they cleaned me up I can still smell the vomit and am very upset. Dan insists, I am fine, but my sister, God bless her, understands what I am trying to say and pipes in and says, "If Erika says she smells vomit, you'd better look closer."

Dan doesn't like my sister and it is obvious. He is getting irritated, but he can tell she is going to be relentless until she has an answer. Finally, he pulls out the liner around my trach and a chunk of vomit falls from my neck. I am beyond disgusted and yet satisfied in showing them I hadn't lost my mind along with my movement. And this went for everything - not just the vomit, all of it. Except for when I was completely looped on meds, I knew exactly what was happening. . and that was often not a good thing.

Dan stoops down, cleans me up, and asks me what my pain level is like. I don't want to take the highest dosage of medication allowed, so I say it's bad but not that bad, but I am lying. (By the way, I don't know why people think that you don't feel pain when you are paralyzed. They are different nerves cells, and while my motor nerves weren't currently working my sensory nerves, which feel things like sheets on your body, were very much alive. I also think the disintegration of the myelin sheath around my nerves was causing me pain as well, it all hurts, who really knows? In any event, Dan knows I am lying and tells me he is giving me the maximum dosage.) I know there are reported cases of Guillain-Barre Syndrome not being that painful, but I definitely fell on the other end of that spectrum. Each case presents differently, which is in part why they call it a syndrome. By definition, a syndrome is a collection of symptoms for which there is no good ideology, cause, or cure. Syndromes are not well understood, even to this day. The usual course of action, therefore, is to treat the symptoms. That is the best they can do.

As one can imagine, my surgery, which had been scheduled for tomorrow morning, is canceled.

Feb. 26, 2001

A new doctor, Dr. Baker, is coming in to see me this morning. He's a gastroenterologist, and they say if anyone can help me, he can. I am awake when he arrives. He is an African American man, about forty years old, with a kind and gentle demeanor. As mentioned, not many people have the ability or the time to read my lips, but he displays both. He talks to me, which is a nice change from most folks, who talk over me or even at me when I am lucky. Most people appear to feel uncomfortable around me and don't even know where to look. Anyway, Dr. Baker empathizes with me and my nausea and is trying to think of what will help. As he is about to leave, I start to make frightening noises through my trach. *What is going on now?* I think Dr. Baker is going to figure it out, but he continues out the door just as I start to vomit again. And again, I start to vomit not just through my mouth, I am vomiting through my trach and I am choking. God, am I sick. Finally, the breathing alarm sounds and a nurse comes rushing in to help me.

I don't know what Dr. Baker thought he knew or didn't know but later that evening Dan comes in and says "Erika, I am sorry but I have to give you more feeding tube fluid through that feeding tube." I can see how awful he feels about the prospective outcome. "I know this is going to make you sick again, but it is the doctor's orders and I have to do this." He does add, "I will stop to extract it as soon as you get uncomfortable."

I try to remain calm. He begins to insert the feeding tube fluid. Shortly after I am so very sick again. Dan then siphons the fluid back out of my stomach. "LEAVE ME ALONE!" I want to scream, but I am too exhausted and drained, physically and emotionally.

Somewhere during all of this my sister comes in and tells me how much her life sucks. She goes on to say she had to get divorced because her husband is gay. I distinctly remember this day as she is drinking a Diet Coke and I am sooo thirsty. I'm also dumbfounded that she is telling me this now, is she trying to tell me we all have problems? I have no idea, but I want her Diet Coke. I can still remember that awful thirst. I could have no oral liquids at all and hadn't for months. Dale had begged her not to bring that Diet Coke in as he knows the situation well; she apparently did not.

Feb. 27 – 28?

Due to the ileus and feeding problems, surgery has been put off indefinitely. We need a fix for this first. I am so weak and sick.

I am being fed through an IV in my arm. It has all the fluids and vitamins my body needs. Apparently, a nutritionist analyzes my blood every day and determines what my nutritional needs are. I am impressed. They tell me this is only a short-term solution and that I need solid nutrition to stay alive, though they haven't figured out how to accomplish this yet.

Well, I think, *you doctors better figure something out.* My thoughts are not of dying: in fact, I don't think death even crosses my mind. I don't think there won't be a solution. I just focus on how to get through each hour, each day.

My favorite cousin, Carolyn, is a nutritionist in Boston. Pretty, smart, and supportive, she has seen me through many difficult times in my life including when Jessica was sick as an infant. Now Carolyn is advising my family via phone, saying "She has to get a J-tube." She explains that a J-tube goes directly into the jejunum in the small intestine. Obviously, she is the only one thinking outside of the box. Using the J-tube would allow them to bypass the ileus with the feeding tube and still give me nutrition.

Days pass and no one in ORMC has caught onto the J-Tube idea. I am losing more and more weight. Being rather thin to begin with, this is not good. In the meantime, the IV fluids keep me alive.

I don't recall being hungry. I only recall being confused, weak, and sick.

Later:

My nurse is in my room, treating me like a number in the grocery store line. I ask, "Am I going to die?" Her response startles me: "Well, Erika, you have had a lot of complications."

What kind of answer is this?

Someone must have made a few phone calls as Dr. Wolfe shows up not long after with a few other doctors to advise me that this may be the end. He says "Erika, there is a very real possibility that you are not going to make it," then adds "Make sure your family is taken care of and your finances are in order." While I appreciate his candor today (I'm sure this was hard to tell a young woman), I didn't appreciate it at all at the time and mouthed "FUCK YOU" to all of them. I wasn't giving in. I would be relentless. My mom, Ron, and Dale were there as well, though I think only Dale and one of the doctors caught the "FUCK YOU" I mouthed.

Feb. 28, 2001

My Aunt Carol is up to visit me. I love my Aunt Carol. We are having a family conference with the doctors to determine which course to take to seal my fate. I am wheeled into the meeting. I feel like I look pretty good (denial can be a great thing), I mean, I am out of bed, which to me, at least, is a big deal. But I am in pain, terrible pain, and exhausted just from sitting.

Dr. Wolfe walks in, joining the doctors already present, including Dr. Geary who is to perform the lung surgery. I try to take control of the situation by asking, "Who is in charge here?" Dr. Wolfe responds that he is the one in charge as my attending physician. I ask where we go from here since the lung surgery has been postponed.

No one wants to answer me. They talk over me and refer to me as a "non-responsive GBS quadriplegic." I am stunned and outraged by both descriptors. Number one, non-responsive, *does this mean non-recovering*, this is bullshit to me. Fuck you and your non-responsiveness/non-recovering; do you know how difficult it is for me to continue breathing each day? Number two just who do you think you are, calling me a quadriplegic? Then I catch myself. *I am a quadriplegic right now but again, FUCK YOU, I will recover!*

Dr. Wolfe is saying how many complications I have had including the ileus and they need to resolve that issue first before working on my lungs. Dr. Wolfe also says I am not motivated enough. Additionally, he says that I should stop using pain medication as that can cause slowed mobility (my ileus) and slowed respiration.

I have never been called non-motivated in my life! I am not happy with this meeting.

Dr. Wolfe stops by my room later. He checks me out and is about to leave when I ask him, "What do I need to do?" He reiterates that I should stop the pain meds. I say I'd rather die if that is my only option, as the pain is too great. I say I will try anything else, but I just can't take the pain. And I can't. I have had two children one with no drugs – as well as broken bones and stitches, but this is different. This is a pain I could never describe.

Apparently, he starts to understand and doesn't fight me anymore on it. He still expresses concern about my respirations while on pain meds, but ultimately is surprised at my eagerness and motivation. However, he says he has never seen me so motivated before, which confuses the hell out of me. Doesn't he understand that it takes every ounce of motivation every day just to stay alive? I am so misunderstood at times. I cannot speak to explain, but I am fighting. I am fighting for my life. I am fighting for my children's lives. I am giving it everything I have.

March 1?, 2001

Plot twist: my mother who has always recognized my pain, wants me to talk with a pain management doctor. I am eager to get whatever help I can for it.

At one point the doctors had told Mom that they were worried I would get addicted and ruin my life. "Well if she lives and needs it," she roared, "we will send her to rehab!"

-Go, Mom!

People look at minuscule things at times. They don't see the forest for the trees. Who cared if I got addicted – I was dying. And I was dying in agony.

Alarmingly, Mom also starts talking about my "final plans."

I say, "You think I am going to die?" She says, "Oh, no, but let's just talk to the doctor and see what he has to say…"

(Later I find out Mom has been driving around with a black dress in the back of her car since this all began.)

Back to the pain management…Dr. Kolles walks in. He is a large man with dark brown hair. He has a gentle manner and at first I think I am going to like him. He has a pretty assistant with him. I think her name is Jean. They say they can get me better pain medication. Dilaudid, in a pump form. Dilaudid is like morphine but eight times stronger. They are excited that they can administer via a pump; now, the question arises: how I am going to press the pump?! This is laughable.

I am told I can request to have one of the nurses press the pump for me but that would require hitting a call button which I can't do either!

Finally, they have a solution. They rig a better call button. It is a big ball by my head. As I am able to turn my head I can ring the bell by hitting the ball and alert someone at the nurses' station. (Up to this point I have had no way to press a call button, no way to ask for help. However, if the ventilator stopped and I stopped breathing an alarm would sound. Not the best way to ask for assistance.)

This sounds good in theory, however, there are many problems they have not thought of that I soon encounter. Usually, some well-meaning aide will move the rigged call-button while bathing me or doing some other necessary evil and forget to move it back.

Recently they had tried giving me some kind of apparatus that I was to blow into to alert the nurses, but for whatever reason it leaves me without a TV and believe me, I need the distraction. (By the way, this issue never gets fixed).

Dr. Kolles says that he is not going to say I am going to die but, "You're sick enough that you could." *What kind of answer is that??* I decide that I hate this man, not only because of his ambivalent response, but because like my mother he wants me to sign a bunch of papers that would financially protect my kids and screw my husband.

They all think I am going to die. I can't stand to hear this. I don't want to die. I love life, especially my life.

I ask to talk to Mom alone. I ask her why she thinks I will die. She denies this, saying it's just that I've been so sick…blah blah blah. Frustrated and heartbroken, I just want to be alone.

Later:

Dr. Kolles' wonderful assistant, Jean, returns to my room for some reason. I hear her say (though I do not recall whether she was talking to Mom or a nurse), "This woman is not going to die. She has a beautiful light all around her." I know I do. I can feel it. It feels like a bright crystal mosaic in my room with me, and I find it strange that she senses it too. Perhaps this is God…perhaps Jesus…perhaps love, but I am being carried. I recall having this sense when I saw my father's dead body in his hospital bed years before; there was a greater presence in the room.

March 1, 2001

I am crying inside. Jessica has her first-grade play tonight, and she has been asking me for two weeks if I will be well enough to go. With my heart aching, I said, "Well, honey, I don't think Mommy will be out of the hospital by then."

I ask Mom to write a letter to Jessica from me. I know my sister has promised Jessica that she will be at the play, but I don't think this makes up for Mommy's absence. Later, I find out that my sister wasn't able to make it either. My poor little girl! I'm so happy she has a fighting spirit, but this all has to hurt her as well.

My friend, the male nurse whose name I cannot remember, comes to visit, as he does frequently. Apparently, he floats between ORMC and Lucerne and has taken the time to find me.

After telling me about his wife and child, he tells me I will be fine. I repeat it back to him and thank God for someone positive. He tells me he will stop by every day possible, if only for a few minutes. It seems God places angels in our path when we need them most.

I have a new nurse today, a kind, heavyset woman named Karen. She asks if I'd like to get out of the rolling therapeutic hospital bed I am currently in and get into a regular one. The rolling bed rolls me from side to side like I am in a boat. It is supposed to reduce the risk of pneumonia which I've had several times already, but it is extremely uncomfortable and impossible to sleep in. Needless to say, I am ecstatic to get out of this boat of a bed and into a regular bed! My enthusiasm is dampened by the realization that they will have to move me, and it will most likely hurt – a lot!!

They have had to move me a couple of times, like when they tried to get me into a chair; the pain was almost unbearable. Furthermore, they usually have to unhook the ventilator temporarily until I am moved and then hook it back up. As one might guess, this is absolutely terrifying to me.

The nurse says she wants to put the order in, and the bed should arrive at some point tonight. So, now my eagerness has turned to fear…awaiting the inevitable move.

Dale arrives that night to find me in my new bed. The process was as horrible as expected, but I am so proud! He will be happy, I think. To me, this means that I am getting better.

March 2, 2001

The physical therapists come into my room to work with me. I am so grateful for their company. I am always grateful to not be alone. I fear the loneliness. I always fear that the ventilator will fail, and no one will help me.

The therapists are young girls in their twenties. They remember me from when I was at ORMC before. They say I am so much better than the last time they saw me. I am thrilled, though I don't remember much of my previous stay. I keep trying to keep them in my room talking (mouthing words). They are polite enough to try with me, but they have work to do and move on all too soon.

As I lay in my new bed, I realize I can move the fingers on my right hand!! It's not a lot of movement but it's definitely movement. Finally, the miracle of a small healing! Initially, they had told me movement would come back but then they all seemed to give up hope.

I can't wait to show Jessica! I think I might even be able to attempt to play checkers with her (This was a very far cry from reality, but I was grasping at straws of encouragement).

Later I show my mother and Ron that I can move my fingers. They applaud loudly. Ron may have even cried a little.

March 3, 2001

I am bored. What to do? I don't know where anyone is. Mom will probably be coming but who knows when. Karen is taking care of me again today, but I have not seen her in a while. I think the ICU nurses only have two patients each, so I am surprised when I am left unattended for what seems to me to be a very long time.

I lay quietly for a while until I can't take it anymore. I am uncomfortable and scared. I have no idea why I am more agitated than usual, but I can't breathe well and am panicking. I start to make a clicking noise with my mouth. No one responds. I get louder and louder (*I later find out that many patients who can't talk will use this as a way to get someone's attention*).

Karen comes in and says in an exasperated voice "I'll be back in just a minute."

More time passes, breathing is harder, and I am certain that I need to be suctioned. Karen doesn't return. No one comes. I begin clicking again. I click as loud as I can. After what seems to be about ten minutes of this Karen storms in and snaps, "What do you need?" Now, it is not as if I can answer, so she will have to slow down, read my lips, ask questions et cetera. However, this doesn't happen. Instead, she says, "You need to learn patience!" If that wasn't enough, she then adds, "Perhaps God has given you this illness because you were not a patient, pleasant person before. Sometimes He gives people illnesses for certain reasons, and you are a demanding person."

She quickly fixes my bed, so now I am not only alone, I am alone and horrified. She didn't even suction me which is what I needed.

I start to cry. I feel so terribly hopeless and helpless, not to mention burdensome. I lay quietly crying, wanting to die.

By the time Mom and Ron arrive I am despondent. I tell them I am sorry to be such a burden and then manage to share what happened with Karen. I start to cry and they cry too, especially Ron, which touches me so much. They give me hope to go on and then immediately get that nurse removed from my case.

March 4, 2001

I have a leak in my trach tube. Again, it takes a lot of complaining about shortness of breath before they finally pay attention and discover the cause. Then, suddenly, EVERYONE is concerned!! They bring in some specialist who puts a balloon on the side of my trach. It seems to help, though they have to adjust it several times. Mom is there asking questions, to which a tall, brown-haired nurse keeps telling her (and ignoring me) that I am fine. I kept thinking, *Fine for you, you are breathing on your own!*

When Mom says she is hungry and is going to get a sandwich, the nurse tells her to go ahead and that I will be fine. I am not as convinced. I hate to complain but I am really scared. The new contraption doesn't seem too secure, and I think they should get something more reliable before they all abandon me, but Mom says she is going to get the sandwich and come right back. She is insistent and leaves.

"Right back" feels like forever. When she eventually returns, I ask what took so long and she says she decided to eat in the cafeteria as she needed some time. I know I am in for a long "look at all I've done for you" talk if I say anything so I stay quiet. I hate this dependency. And I was right to be fearful of the new contraption; respiratory had to be called in for a better fix.

Later:

It is late afternoon. Mom is going and it will be hours before Dale arrives. As usual I am bored (there's not even TV to watch, the TV was always problematic), worried, and alone again.

Two nice nurses stop in and tell me they are going to give me a PICC line. When I indicate that I don't know what this is, they explain that it is a line in my arm with a tube that runs all the way up to my heart. It allows them to draw blood easily. My veins are collapsing from the overuse of IV medications and treatments, and the staff has found getting blood from me to be quite frustrating. I want to remind them that it is frustrating for all of us!

I am just thrilled to have company again; little did I know it wasn't going to be a fun visit.

Then it starts, with them repeatedly stabbing my arm. They confer and try the other arm. Again, stab, stab, stab. They are growing frustrated and concerned. I am beginning to grow a little alarmed but also feeling too drained to care. After working for more than an hour and a half with no success, they decide to put in a midline in my neck instead. I am confused. I think this means I will have it forever but, again, I am now too tired to care. *(It would take more than two years out of the hospital to figure out where the scar on the left side of my neck was from.)*

When Dale arrives, he is horrified. He says there is so much blood it looks like I've been shot!

March 5 , 2001

I have received the J-tube through the PEG tube. At least that is what Mom has told me.

I am not tolerating the J-tube very well. They must keep pumping bile out from my gallbladder. Apparently, they start to give me Ativan for my anxiety which I am not happy about at all. I think, *Don't drug me so I am not bothered by the problem – just fix the problem!!*

March 7, 2001

My physical therapist wants to put me in a chair. Just the thought of it scares me but the huge, muscular nurse promises that he can handle me; there will be no pain nor a need to disconnect the vent. He says, "Trust me Erika" – boy, I've heard that one before! I would love to trust him, to trust anyone, to trust anything but since the unbelievable has happened in my life, trust has gone out the window.

So now I am in the chair, God it hurts to be moved and takes so much energy to sit. And yes, the ventilator alarm goes off, several times!! I am alarmed even on the damn Ativan – like, who wouldn't be? So, please stop telling me to trust you; no one knows what to do with me. People who work in the hospital stop by to see the woman with the worst case of Guillain-Barre they have ever seen. I am a new phenomenon, so just stop making promises you can't keep.

IVIG (Immunoglobulin given intravenously) is supposed to stop the disease process. Never worked for me. So, then they gave me plasmapheresis; I received something like seventeen rounds of that. Nothing has worked. Now, two months later, a little movement in my fingers and we are all thrilled. Doctors have seen nothing like it. As one can imagine, this is not a good feeling.

Mom arrives and tells me she is seeing a therapist. Here I am in survival mode, with my mental state totally on hold. I can't even think of my kids. All my energy is focused on living, so a therapist is the furthest thing from my mind. Mom, however, apparently needs support. As I look back, I'm glad she sought it out, but at the moment I was just thinking, *Oh shit, now she is falling apart...*

I have wondered how she and Dale are getting along without me as a buffer. I wonder if Dale's work habits are better, but I am too afraid to ask. *(Remember, I am in absolute self-protection mode. No other problems, please!!)* I appease myself thinking they are okay. I never ask how they are managing financially. I wonder if I will have any money left, but this is a fleeting thought and obviously not important at the moment.

Mom wants to know if she can bring Jessica to her therapist. I don't want Jess to go! I really think she is too young and shouldn't be pushed into talking about anything she is not prepared to talk about. She is my kid and I will address it with her when I am out. My mom has always been very pro-counseling and therapy. I have always been and, as a licensed mental health counselor, obviously still am. Still, I am hesitant with kids. Kids are hard, and sometimes it can do more damage than good unless you have a fantastic therapist that specializes in child psychology. In the end, I tell Mom she can take Jessica for a session but only if she and the therapist will take Jessica's lead. And yet again, I have little say. I must just be grateful, and I am but geez, so much I have to let go of…all control; everything from taking a bowel movement to my kid's mental health.

March 8, 2001

Dale comes to visit me in the middle of the day. I can't figure it out. I don't ask why and am just grateful for the company. Nighttime comes too quickly and passes too slowly. I watch the nurses outside my room, hustling around. I see them go back to the break room. I can see that Coke machine from my room, beckoning me like a mirage in a desert. I love Coke, and I am so thirsty.

My vent alarm goes off again and there is no help in sight. Finally, a young male nurse who has a crush on me (or so I think, which amazes me as I am at my absolute worst) comes to my aide. I think, *He is an idiot!* and ask to have him get Dan. He says he can help but I have no confidence in him and as he fumbles around, I must have given him a look that says I mean business because he goes to get Dan. Little do I realize he has managed to reconnect the tube and I am okay.

The darn thing keeps coming off too easily and I am losing confidence in everyone.

March 9, 2001

I am excited to learn I will have the lung surgery. Perhaps now I will get off this stupid vent. I think I hate the vent even more than I hate being paralyzed. There is talk of a lobectomy, but no one has really come clean with me about this. My biggest problem for the moment is that Jonathan needs his first real haircut, and I am not there to either give him one or take him. I am so sad. I want to be home for this. I want to be home for it all.

March 11, 2001

It is a good day. Mom, Ron, and Dale bring the kids and I am so happy to see them all. Doctor Geary stops in to see me. He says I will have the surgery tomorrow morning at 7 a.m. I ask if I should be worried, and he says it is not like removing my tonsils, but it is not open-heart surgery either. I am somehow relieved by this analogy.

(I don't know why I wasn't more worried, but I wasn't. I probably was too sick and too overwhelmed already to add more fears to my plate.)

Jessica and I get to talking. I tell her I'll be home by June. I want to say May, but the word June slips out (*Oddly, this turns out to be a premonition as I would in fact return home in early June.*) I felt like this date was slightly exaggerated, but no one else seemed to agree. I just didn't pay attention to anyone else's opinion.

March 12, 2001

It's early morning, very early. They are all bustling around me, including Mom and Ron, who had spent the night at a special hotel for ORMC patients. It's Ron's birthday, and he is spending it with me. I am happy to have so many visitors...and then I see that Karen, the nurse who was cruel to me is back. Mom notices immediately and the woman is once again removed from my care. Mom was mad!

Mom calms down and so do I. I vaguely remember them praying over and with me. They ask me if I am ready. I am more than ready. This is what will get me off the ventilator, or so I believe. I have no concept of how dangerous it is, nor do I even contemplate what it will mean if the surgery is a failure.

I remember laying in the operating room with the bright lights. I am still awake; *shouldn't I be asleep?* I guess I sleep for a while and fade in and out during the bronchoscopy which happens after the surgery. I remember fighting to stay awake. The surgery is over, and they are moving me back to another room. I can hear some woman saying, "Man, this lady is dry" and I think to myself, *Well, of course I am, I have not been allowed anything to drink for months and am dying of thirst!! I keep telling everyone!!*

I am awake by the time they wheel me back in my room where Mom and Ron are waiting. They are surprised to see me awake already; I am surprised how excruciating the pain is. I remember remarking that no one had told me it would hurt like this. I feel like I have been shot. Regardless, they all say the surgery is a success. I didn't expect anything less.

Dale comes in later to see me. I am still in so much pain, but I am darn glad it is over!!

March 15, 2001

I have another nurse from hell, or maybe he is a respiratory therapist. He is like a drill sergeant, telling me the only way to get off the vent is to fight it. He keeps trying to put me off the vent for extended periods of time. I am not ready. I have been on the vent for one hundred days and I am frightened. I have had some bad experiences here and I think this man might be what finally kills me!

March 18, 2001

The respiratory therapist from hell has decided I must be off the ventilator all day and he will put me back on it at night. I alternately love and hate this man. I am so pleased to be off the vent, so scared to be off it, and yet still I am so afraid I'll never get off it entirely.

March 20, 2001

I am shocked when Mom comes in to tell me she has moved out. I hadn't realized things between her, and Dale had deteriorated to that extent. Or, one could say I had chosen to ignore the subject entirely. Of course I had noticed their bickering, and it is all too much. I am still not breathing on my own…can someone give me a break?

I know both Mom and Dale can be very difficult in very different ways, and I'm angry with both of them for being so self-centered that they couldn't work something out for the kids! Shouldn't it be about what is best for Jessica and Jonathan? This certainly is not what is best for them.

I feel like Mom wants me to side with her. I can't think of all this right now. I am still too weak and trying to live, and possibly recover.

March 19, 2001

I am off the vent all day! I have had company. Mom, Ron, and then our pastor came to visit. As he leaves, I begin to feel again like I can't breathe. I communicate what's happening to Mom, who says I must go back on the ventilator. It is before the scheduled time which is both frustrating and terrifying. I feel like a failure and fear I will never get off this vent. And it doesn't help that I have overheard staff talk of the real possibility of me living my life out in a rehabilitation center for individuals that can't get off the ventilator.

Mom is so wonderful. She reassures me that it is okay to take a temporary slide backward sometimes. Not one to normally cut myself slack, I fear she is wrong but have no choice at this point. It is back on the vent or imminent death.

March 20, 2001

I do get off the vent! I still have the trach to help me breathe and it still needs cleaning, but no ventilator! The trach collar, which is as fashionable as one would imagine, goes around the trach to hold it in place so humidified air can be blown into the trachea to aide in breathing. I need the trach collar as I am still not pulling enough air in by myself – yet!

I am so excited and proud. I want to show off to all these stupid nurses that told me to give up, that "sometimes, we just need to let go" – who thought I would never make it. And let's not forget the other nurses who were just plain horrible to me.

I want to show them all that while I have not yet made it to full-on recovery (I am still paralyzed), I AM OFF THE VENTILATOR!

I am being transferred upstairs to PCU. PCU is where I came from originally and hated it. However, today I am winning. Faye, the nurse who made special trips into my room to encourage me to let go and die, to "just go in peace" is there, and I want to say, "See ya, BITCH I did it, and, moreover, "FUCK YOU! I'm gonna live!

Tye, Vincent's wife, is here to see me too! Vincent is one person who had GBS even worse than me. He was unable to open his eyes for a number of months and was on the vent even longer. Perhaps it would have been helpful if he had been treated at ORMC. They all seem so lost with me.

Tye tells me it is going to be okay, and I want to believe her but it's hard when her husband is still so sick. I am scared but determined to keep the faith. Today is a good day. I will focus on that. I have left the ICU and am off the ventilator. Miracles do happen. I had many moments of thinking I would die in the ICU and several days when I cried out to let me go be with my deceased father. It was tough, to say the least.

Later:

I have arrived upstairs. It is quiet. I wait for Mom. I wait for someone. Anyone? Where is everyone? I still can't hit the buzzer for help. Will I die now in the PCU? Does anyone know my history? Does anyone know I am just off the vent? HELP!

Mom comes in and says a few choice words about the insurance company she has been dealing with and then she is gone again.

A young respiratory nurse is walking by, and I make my clicking noise to get her attention. However, now she is angry. She has an order and is on her way to execute it and she will get to me when she gets to me.

It is going to be a long night.

March 21, 2001

The morning is great. I have been moved to a regular room and the sun is shining. A nurse comes in and says she is here to bathe me. I say, "I want to wash my hair" and, to my surprise, she agrees.

Mom has washed my hair for me a few times while in the ICU (using only a sponge) but most of the time I just wore it in braids all over my head. There was nothing else to do with my remaining long blonde locks *(I say remaining as much of my hair has been cut off although I don't know it at this point.)*

I am so excited about the prospect of getting my whole head wet instead of just sponged down! I don't remember it all, however, I do remember feeling like I had grossly moved up on the food chain! I am in a regular room with clean hair!!

Later:

Dr. Bass, my pulmonologist, and several other doctors come to meet with me and Mom about my plan of care. To date, I still have not passed the swallow study and remain on the feeding tube unable to take any food or liquid orally. I remember months earlier, when after another swallow study they said that I had not only failed, I had "grossly, beyond margin, failed."

Today I ask Dr. Bass, "When can I drink on my own?" Mom and the nurses again remind me that I have repeatedly failed the swallow study.

Dr. Bass, God love him, replies, "Well, let's make this the swallow study!" He turns to me and says, "Erika, what would you like to drink?" I immediately reply, "I want a Coke, a Coca-Cola!" Dr. Bass, with no hesitation, says, "Get her a Coke!"

The nurse brings in a Coke. In retrospect this could have killed me, I could have aspirated into my lungs, but I guess Dr. Bass thought it was worth the risk and knew how much I had suffered and was all about treating me like a human being.

I am so pleased with the Coke. I am so thirsty. I haven't had a sip of anything for three months. I chug half the can of Coke without stopping. It is a victory I will never forget.

March 22, 2001

After much conversation with the insurance company, it is deter-mined that I have to leave ORMC and am being sent back to the hospital from hell, Lucerne (my experience). Mom is furious that they are sending me back to that insanity and chaos. I am not thrilled either but have come to accept so many unacceptable things…I am breathing and drinking. I can take it.

I arrive at Lucerne. They all remember me. I don't remember them. I was too sick last time I was here. I am not now, though, and can't wait to show off that I can breathe on my own and now even talk!! Watch out!

I tell the nurse how much better I am now and that I will soon go home. Although I am still mostly paralyzed and can only move my right hand a little, breathing and talking is hope!

March ? , 2001

Today is going to be my best day in the hospital yet!! My friend, the man who used to always come by and visit me in ORMC (and Lucerne on occasion), is my nurse. I am thrilled. This is the best care I've received in the hospital. Today I do not feel afraid!

Then I find out I won't be able to stay here either. Appar-ently, though paralyzed I am not sick enough for the hospital anymore. I must be transferred to either a nursing home or a rehabilitation center.

Mom and Ron look all over town for a place for me to go. They examine nursing home after nursing home. They even bring me with them for a tour (oh, that was fun). I couldn't even begin to take it in. I remember thinking, *There is no way in hell I am going to go here,* but I say nothing. I am at everyone's mercy.

Even Mom looks sad. I know she can't picture putting me in a nursing home and in all honesty I can't either. I know she feels as if she is giving up on me; however, I am not well enough to go to a rehab center. I wouldn't be able to keep up with the necessary requirements. So, Mom is in full-on business mode.

I am sure something will change Mom doesn't seem so sure. I am off the vent but still catheterized, almost completely paralyzed and on a trach collar but am still convinced I am NOT going to a nursing home.

Miracles do happen. Mom meets Beth, liaison to Dr. Wolfe and Dr. Brums (my attending physician and partner). She is able to pull all sorts of strings and get me into Florida Hospital Rehabilitation Center. I would have gone to Lucerne rehabs, but a colleague of Dr. Wolfe's says I am not motivated enough. I cannot believe I am hearing this craziness once again. I want to scream, "Being paralyzed does not equal a lack of motivation!!"

Furthermore, it is questionable whether or not I am even ready to be moved out of ICU – this, according to the results of a chest X-Ray dated March 26, 2001, per my mom's notes. I am also still in terrible physical pain, for which I've been on massive amounts of medication. That is to say nothing of the emotional pain that, again, has had to take a back burner. I must get well. That is my motto, all else can be dealt with later.

My insurance will only pay for sixty days of rehabilitation. Help me, Lord, I can't exactly do the stationary bike. Anyway, this pushes the nursing home off by a couple of months.

March 30, 2001

Here I am, packed up, ready to go, and terrified. I am not in good enough shape for the rehab, but I can't stay at the hospital because of the insurance, nor will I go to a nursing home yet. The second part of that statement I am not sure about, but Mom explains this is the best choice, so I go with it and am being transported to Florida Hospital Rehabilitation.

I am told they exercise six hours a day at this facility and I wonder, as I can barely breathe on my own, *How will I do this?* Anyway, I am on my way just the same. As with everything else that has occurred over the past three-plus months, I am a passive recipient. I don't have a lot of choices. I would like to throw up my arms and scream, "I AM GOING HOME!" but my arms don't work.

Chapter 6

Rehabilitation – Am I Ready?

March 31, 2001

I am transferred to Florida Hospital Rehab. Mom says it is a godsend. I am not so sure. I know the nursing staff will be smaller, meaning I will have to wait even longer to get anything. I am newly off the vent and concerned (very concerned) about my breathing.

The hot, hot Florida sun burns my eyes as I am brought outside to the ambulance. In the past three months I have only been outside for trips to and from Lucerne to ORMC which are approximately two blocks from each other. I miss being outside. I love Florida, and I am reminded I am missing the best months of the year. Spring is beautiful in Florida.

The ride over takes forever, and my anxiety grows. We arrive and I watch as Mom talks to the admitting nurse, thinking, *"Hey, I can finally talk, let me say something!" I was so eager to talk for myself!*

I don't think they have ever seen anyone as sick as I am, and that worries me. I am wheeled into a room with four beds, all of them empty. This is just as well as I don't want a roommate, but I'm confused and upset when they put me back in the corner bed. I am alone and isolated again, only now I can't even see the hall.

Please don't hide me, I still can't move! Why are they putting me way back here?

April 1, 2001

A wonderful blonde assistant comes into my room the following morning. Too bad I can't remember her name now (perhaps Karen or Carrie?). Anyway, she is not a nurse, just a loving soul who helps me get some sips of orange juice at my request.

Now I normally hate orange juice, but I am currently so thirsty for orange juice over ice (I still drink it this way to this day!) I still have my feeding tube as I can't tolerate too much oral consumption. I either get sick or I get exhausted. Chewing and swallowing are quite the workout for me.

Carrie asks me if she can do anything else for me. I want my hair washed. It's been at least two weeks since my last hair washing in the hospital, and I feel gross. Mom reminds me of the initial stages of Guillain-Barre, when I went for months without my hair being washed. Back then everyone was too busy keeping me alive (priorities, I suppose.)

When I was at ORMC, my friend Terri came in to assist with my hair. Though I had no idea at the time, my hair had apparently been the topic of many discussions. Terri, who was a hair stylist, was a big help.

When I was first put on the ventilator, I fought it (in fact, as mentioned earlier, I had even bitten one of the nurses, hard). To keep me from biting anyone else they placed a mask of sorts

(Dale said it resembled a hockey mask) over my face. Unaware of how important hair is to this dying woman, they used something similar to duct tape (as mentioned in an earlier entry) to keep the mask on and wrapped it around my long blonde tresses.

I would then bang my head from side to side out of sheer frustration of the whole experience. I do remember this. My head was all I could move, and I was furious.

Some sweet precious soul decided it was all too much and they gave me one of the "date rape" drugs so I would forget the torment of it all. Unfortunately for Dale, the experience would remain forefront in his memory. *For years his eyes would well up with tears as he spoke about it.*

Back at ORMC, at one point after the tracheotomy, Mom had asked Terri to come in and work her magic to get the tape and tangles out of my hair. After hours of trying to comb through my hair Terri gave up and cut a good chunk off the back. They did not tell me; I could only see the front and they planned it that way (for which I am very grateful; I had lost so much already). They wanted to preserve as much of my identity, and pride, as they could.

April ?, 2001

Some team of special nurses comes in to change my PICC line. Just like when they first put it in at ORMC, they are having difficulty as my veins are collapsing from the continual use and the lack of nutrition. This time Mom is with me and is frustrated by their attempts (and probably scared as well, wondering if they know what they are doing).

But the sun is out, and I have a window view. It feels so wonderful to have the sun on my face and be able to breathe with only a little help. *Keep stabbing away,* I think, *I am in no hurry.*

As the day wears on and the nursing team leaves, I begin to feel sick to my stomach. This is not new, but it is intense. I am supposed to start therapy today. I want to start therapy today. I only have sixty days here and every second counts. I know they (the therapists) think I'm just whining. They come in and say they want to start anyway. I can't; I start to cry and then I start to vomit.

Holly, my physical therapist, won't give up as I stop vomiting. She decides she can still do some passive exercises with me ("passive" meaning I can't move but Holly moves part of my body.) My body really hasn't moved in three months, and it is very stiff. The exercises are very painful, though it feels good that someone is trying to see me improve, that there is hope, something new is happening. I grow to love Holly immensely.

April ?, 2001

They are having a meeting this morning to discuss my progress and treatment plan. My loving husband won't be here but everyone else under the sun will be. The conference includes Mom, me (of course), the physical therapists, the occupational therapists, and even John (the social worker). Let me not forget to mention that my care has now been transferred to Dr. Creamer. *(He will become my doctor for many years to come, for which I am very grateful.)*

Dr. Creamer outlines a plan of attack. He is very concerned about my bedsore, which he calls a decubitus. I have not heard too much about this bedsore. I can't even really feel the pain, it is all so painful. It is hard to differentiate one pain from another.

However, Dr. Creamer is adamant about making this a priority. It is very severe, he says, and could potentially require surgery in which the skin would be grafted from elsewhere on my body.

I am convinced it can't be all that bad, *I am in denial.* The instructions remain that I am to avoid laying on my back, although this doesn't really hurt or hurt any more than anything else. They also use a heat lamp on occasion. There is so much else to be done with me. The nurses must be tiring, I think.

I only remember Dr. Geary discussing bedsores, or my bed-sore, when he performed the lung surgery. Obviously, the nurs-ing staff at ORMC and Lucerne were not too worried about it, but again, perhaps it was a ranking of priorities. When someone is dying are we worried about bedsores?

Anyway, I am glad someone has a plan, and I am ready to work. I have always been a hard worker. Hearing I have to work hard is right up my alley. Hearing that I have to sit and do noth-ing (in this case, lay there and do nothing) is excruciating.

April 6, 2001

My feeding tube (the J-tube intervention) has flown south or popped out. So, Dr. Shrine, who has an excellent reputation, has been called in to reinsert it. He does an endoscopic procedure to evaluate the situation.

He feels he needs to try to reinsert it with some sort of wire, but it doesn't work. I don't recall going through this type of pro-cedure to have it inserted but who listens to me anyway?

The defunct J-tube means several things. I am back to no food and feel very nauseous again. Additionally, in the rehab we don't have IV medications, so I am taking copious amounts of oxy-contin (in addition to everything else I am taking) on an empty stomach. *Who wouldn't be nauseous?* Worse still, the oxycontin causes me to hallucinate. Like my previous hallucinations, they are so vivid, and I have a hard time differentiating them from reality. I get so scared. Sometimes I feel like I am going crazy.

A lovely African American lady is my nurse today. She sings to me and doesn't mind that I ring the call bell frequently. They have now placed a large button next to my head, and if I turn my head I can call for the nurse myself, just like at ORMC. But again, often it is misplaced. Then the struggle is very real.

I later hallucinate that this nurse is nailing me into a coffin to bury me alive. Doesn't take a dream interpreter to figure this one out.

April 7, 2001

I have met with everyone and now I want to go back to ORMC. I want to go back on the vent. I can't breathe. Mom is gone and Dale isn't here either. I need to be suctioned; something is wrong. I ring the bell, but no one comes. I need to go back to the hospital. This is way too much for me. I am crying.

John, the social worker, stops in. He, of course, is not responding to the call light. He is just there to visit. I tell him I can't breathe, and he wants to chat. I get angry and finally he says he will try to find someone to help me. Social workers are great, but feelings are secondary to breathing…again priorities. And this is my truth: life first.

I lay there alone again for quite a long time. I think that I am going to die, and they all are just too busy to care.

Like an angel from heaven, in walks my friend Cathy Andrews. She is a physician herself and I just feel relieved in her presence. I think she brought me lollipops; it doesn't matter, she is here. I tell her how scared I am to be off the vent and that I need to be suctioned. To put it in perspective, when a person needs to be suctioned it feels like they are drowning in their own mucus. Breathing becomes more and more shallow, and it feels like a heavy weight is sitting on your chest.

I need to add that they don't like to suction you. Suctioning is performed by inserting a small vacuum-like tube into your trach opening in your neck and carefully sucking the secretions from your lungs. They try to move the vacuum wand all over your lung area without causing damage to your lungs or otherwise causing damage to the tissue. It is not only tedious work for them, but also potentially dangerous and can easily cause infection each time they insert the wand.

I can't remember if anyone came in to suction me or not. What I do remember is Cathy telling me about her bible study, which is relaxing and helps me to focus on the fact that Dale would come soon. Mom calls, and Cathy says that I am "very nervous."

Nighttime

Two wonderful nurses arrive for the 11 p.m. shift. For the life of me, I can't remember their names. They know I am scared. One of the nurses even sits by my bed. They tell me they are going to give me something for the pain.

The pain has been terrible since I have been here. As mentioned, there are no IV pain meds and trying to control the pain has been a challenge. The oxycontin and hallucinations are no fun, and, furthermore, they don't take the pain away, they just terrify me. So, they are experimenting with pills here (not that I can swallow them); they crush them up and put them in my feeding tube.

The nurses give me my meds and say they will be back later. I think they genuinely care, and I feel better. I go to sleep, but my sleep is not pleasant. I am overmedicated. I dream/hallucinate again that these nurses are burying me alive, but this time in a piano case.

(The next morning the nurses tell me that I kept screaming and crying in my sleep and yelling at them when they would try to calm me. I'm beginning to wonder which is worse, the pain or the hallucinations.)

April 8, 2001

Mom has decided to visit every Monday through Wednesday and then return to her home in Sebring. She says I am busy with therapy and all that type of stuff during the weekdays. I know she is tired and needs a break...*don't we all?*

She has done an incredible job and I am sure she is tired of dealing with this crazy mess, but I feel abandoned and angry. Of course I can't tell her this. She has done so much, and furthermore I am very dependent right now and can't afford to piss people off.

So, I lay alone, can't breathe again. I know I should be suctioned. I hit the call button with my head. They respond and ask what I need. I tell them and they don't come. So of course, I ring again. I wait again but get no response other than, "Yes, we hear you"; "We are coming." I am getting panicky and pissed. I keep ringing.

Finally, Nurse Betty, an older attractive but stern woman enters my room angrily. "You are driving my nurses crazy! WHAT DO YOU NEED?" This is followed by, "This is not going to work here, missy."

I turn my head and look at her. I am just glad I got a response. I say, "I need to be suctioned." She quickly retorts, "I am sure you don't, but okay." As Nurse Betty suctions me she finds I have quite a bit of mucus clogging my lungs. She is surprised, though her only comment is, "I guess you did need to be suctioned this time." Then she walks out.

Holy shit, these are the people who are caring for my life?

April 9, 2001

I am still without the J-tube reinserted; they can't figure out what
ORMC has done as ORMC used the PEG tube and converted it
to a J-tube. In all this confusion I haven't eaten for several days.
No working J-tube means no food for Erika.

I am not hungry, though. I am never hungry. I just hurt and
mostly feel so sick to my stomach.

Mom is really angry that they cannot figure out this procedure. I am frustrated but I have bigger fish to fry. Will I be like
this forever? I know I am authorized to stay in rehab until the
end of May. Each day I watch the local news, noting the date and
calculating how many days I have left. I think about how much
more I will have to recover before I can go home. Worse yet is the
thought that I will not recover before the time limit is up. What
happens then?

April 11, 2001

They have moved me to a smaller room with two beds. The other
bed is empty, and I am glad. I am in no mood for a roommate.
I like the activity of the daytime though and I feel at least that
most people are trying to get me better. I am rarely able to sit
and when I do I feel completely exhausted. Many times, sitting
up makes me vomit so they usually work with me laying down.
Still, you would be amazed at how busy a paralyzed woman's day
can be!

7 a.m.: Wake up

8 a.m.: Get dressed (I hate this part. They always hurt me
unintentionally or perhaps it is intentional – sometimes it's hard
to tell). Socks are a real nuisance as my feet are in so much pain
and the aides are rarely careful and gentle. Sometimes they get
lazy and just don't even change my socks (while this is completely

disgusting and I know it, it is nice to have a break from some additional pain on occasion).

9 to 10:30 a.m.: Physical Therapy

10:45 to 11:45 a.m.: Occupational Therapy.

12 to 1 p.m.: Lunch. Now, this is a joke. I am exhausted by this point. I still have the feeding tube, but they feed me as well. I am so thin. For months I couldn't be weighed except using a Hoyer Lift. I am in the eighty-pound range, so I need all the calories they can get into me. Most days I vomit anything I try to eat orally, then fall asleep with the vomit on me, though sometimes someone helps. I have to wear gloves that will hold the fork for me. As one might imagine, I am not motivated to eat.

1:15 to 2:30 p.m.: Physical Therapy

2:30 to 3:30 p.m.: Occupational Therapy

3:30 to 4:30 p.m.: Recreational Therapy. This is supposed to be fun, however, I am usually annoyed and think it to be a total waste of time.

4:45 p.m.: Return to Room. Someone drops me into my bed. This is not usually a good time. I cough and choke on my own mucus as they try to gently lay me down (most of the time they are gentle at this point…perhaps they can see I am so sick from the day). I usually cry at this time. I usually also ask for pain meds, and I wait for Dale to come help me and comfort me. I watch *Friends* on TV and it makes me laugh, which is good, though I am reminded how far I am from living anything that resembles a normal life.

I never eat dinner; I don't even recall what time they bring it. I am too sick to my stomach. I leave it for Dale, who never has time to eat between work and coming to see me. Also, Dale just really likes to eat (and a lot, I might add). Poor Dale has to feed the kids and then find some loving soul to watch them so he can come up to see me. Luckily, we have friends from the church and neighbors that have really stepped up.

On the rare occasion when he cannot find a sitter, Dale brings the kids in with him. The kids, when they come, are bored within a matter of minutes, plus their energy level is way too high for me. I think it is very hard for Jessica to see me this way, so when she comes she usually focuses on TV.

When Dale doesn't bring the kids he always wants to call them and have me say hi. This is so hard for me; I need to sound positive and happy but I am ill and can't hold the phone. Additionally, it makes me start to worry about them and I know I have to be one hundred percent focused on recovering. This is not the time to be sappy. All that will get fixed if I get better and that is what I am here to do.

April 12th , 2001

I am tired and working hard. I am still at odds with the bitchy Nurse Betty, who unfortunately is the head nurse on the floor. *(I recall telling her my pulse ox was too low (I was always very concerned about my oxygen levels), and that witchy nurse rolled her eyes at me!! I then tried to hit her with my right arm, but as only my fingers worked that did not go as planned. It was lucky for her and most likely lucky for me as well.)*

April 13, 2001

They are getting me up for PT now. They fasten me to my wheelchair so I won't fall out and wheel me down with the rest of the slobs. I am by far one of the youngest in the rehab. Most folks are stroke victims. I soon recognize the haircut of all the stroke victims. Their hair is long in the front and shaved in the back.

(The funny part is that my haircut resembles this, except that I don't know it (see the earlier entry about the haircut I received from my friend Terri.) Funny how judgmental we can be, even when we are all struggling with this human condition called life. Some struggle more than others, but oftentimes we do not see ourselves as we are. As much as I believe we should be humble and one amongst many, I praise God that at this time I wasn't thinking that way. I had no idea how sick I still was and how many odds are against me. I push, I think I am different. I am getting better! I insist.)

There are a few kids in here too. This is such a heartbreak – have they even had a chance to live? A young kid who does PT with me has had a brain bleed and he is perhaps seven or eight years old. I hear him as they try to move his muscles. He is howling in pain and doesn't understand. It is almost too much to bear.

My attitude is, I will endure any pain to get better. I don't care, push me. The difference is that I am older and know why they are hurting me. The kids just know they are hurting them with no understanding of a greater payoff. I wonder if it is more difficult for parents to see their child in pain or for young children to have a parent disappear into the depths of an incredible illness. I have no answer to that one.

Speaking of kids, it will soon be Easter. I instruct my mother to get plenty of Easter goodies for my babies including stuffed bunnies etc. Mom always thinks I do too much for my kids, I think they are God's greatest gift to me and they need all the support they can get right now. What are a few extra presents? It is the least I can do, and it is in fact all I can do. I still can't even hug them! If I was home, it would be so much different. We would go to church, wear special Easter outfits, have a big ham, jellybeans, and an Easter egg hunt. But for today Mom will help me and the kids will accept what is. Jessica had to celebrate her seventh birthday without me. That's enough heartbreak to kill a person, so I mentally can't even go there. I pray God has His hands on my children's heads. God has no grandchildren; I must remember this.

Life has been forever changed for our family.

April 15, 2001

It's Easter! A new beginning, a remembrance of God's grace. I wake up early and am thankful for all the love and prayers that have surrounded me. I feel very carried by my family and friends, many of whom visit frequently. They have loved me through my ugliest, hardest moments.

I always thought I had to be perfect to be loved, but here I am – no makeup, hair an absolute trainwreck, totally paralyzed in my hospital gown, and they keep coming. I am amazed.

Mom, Ron, Dale, and the kids usually visit on Sundays, but I am especially excited today. The kids are dressed in beautiful Easter outfits given to them by some friends of ours from our church. Jessica looks so pretty and Jonathan so handsome. They are such great kids!

Mom has brought everything, including a pink bunny for me!! It is a great day!! We might all just get out of this.

April 16, 2001

Holly, my most wonderful physical therapist, has me down in the gym. She is pushy, but she is also amazing, patient, and encouraging. She wants me to get well. I can feel how much she cares.

She puts me on the workout table. She tells me to try to move my legs. I am thinking she is out of her mind. She continues, saying that as I am lying flat with no resistance, I might be able to move them. AND THEN I DO!! Not a lot of movement, but definite movement!

I am excited but immediately feel like a swimmer who's trying to cross the ocean and gets a bad cramp at the half-mile mark. Holly reminds me that it is one step at a time. Okay, I'll take it. Besides now I am so tired. Everything makes me so tired. I will go back to my room and sleep knowing that I have hit a milestone.

April 17, 2001

Dale comes in for dinner – my dinner, to be exact. It was served a long time ago and just sat there waiting for him. I can't eat. Dale is so funny; he raves about how great the food is. I know he says this about all food he eats, which makes me laugh. He says nightly, "Oh, Erika, this is absolutely the best blah blah blah, you should have some." I am just happy he is there.

They had found some strawberry smoothies in the cafeteria that I like. The smoothies are nice and cold and go down easy. I will definitely eat these and will ask for them nightly.

While Dale is eating and I am having my smoothie, Mom calls with the kids. Since she has moved out, she has been watching them once or twice a week for Dale so he can come and see me. Anyway, she always has me talk to the kids as well. As mentioned before, this is so hard for me. I don't really have the strength to pretend I am okay, but I am trying to be a good Mommy so I do try to talk.

April 18, 2001

Dr. Hain, my new pulmonologist, checks on me daily. He comes in and smiles. He asks how I am doing, and I always say fine.

Well, today he comes in and says, "Let's get rid of that trach, huh?" I am shocked. I say, "No, I can't breathe." He tells me they will first switch to a smaller trach and then remove it altogether. He really is not going to take no for an answer. I am terrified and comply, thinking something w_ll happen between now and Friday (my projected date to take it out).

They also plan on taking out my urinary catheter. I should be thrilled but I am not. I am scared. I haven't been able to rely on my own body functioning the way it should for well over three months now and it seems like a huge leap of faith to do all this at once.

April 19, 2001

I told everyone I know (and some I don't) what is to transpire on Friday. John, my assigned therapist whom I have had disdain for up until this point, comes in to see me. John says he will be there during the procedure with me. I am deeply touched and take him up on it.

Now, it is not that I really hate John, I just hate the role he plays in this (dealing with my emotions). I hate that he wants to know how I feel. I feel like hell, I am so distressed and depressed I'd like to die, but I can't let myse_f feel. I am amazed anyone would ask. How else do they expect me to feel?

I can't focus on my feelings now. I have to focus on getting better. I will focus on my feelings later. I am angry and do not want to make him feel useful."

But I *do* need him. I need any help I can get. I'm scared. What if I die? I don't want to die; do they know what they are doing? Blind faith and terror can exist at the same time. This is what they call courage.

April 21, 2001

Show time. It's 3 p.m. and we are ready to rock and roll. Dr. Hain is right on time. John is here and so is my faithful mother.

I hate not being able to breathe. I hate all of this.

Dr. Hain leans my head back and pulls on the trach. "There, it's out," he announces. I try to talk but air is escaping from the freshly opened trach hole and I don't make any sound. Dr. Hain covers the hole and I say, "Hey, this isn't too bad." Dr. Hain says he has to put the smaller one in. I say, "Forget it, I'll just deal with this. I'm tired of being afraid."

I knew that if he put in the smaller trach I would have to live through the same fear when it was time to remove that one as well. I hate fear so let's just move on now. This is a red-letter day for Erika! Yay! I am trach-free and breathing on my own!

April 22, 2001

They are now getting ready to pull the urinary catheter. Supposedly, I am ready to retrain my bladder so I can pee on my own – not as easy as it sounds after three-plus months of using a catheter. Retraining my bladder means that each time I urinate, the nurses have to check to see if I have released all of the urine. This is done by ultrasound.

If there is still a significant amount of urine (or more than they would like to see), they will have to straight cath me, meaning they insert a tube through my urethra into my bladder and empty the rest of the urine. It is not pleasant but necessary. If too much urine is left in the bladder, it can cause a terrible UTI and even lead to sepsis.

Sometimes they don't check and other times they are too busy to straight cath. So, this bladder retraining is neither really regimented nor well organized.

(Looking back, I clearly didn't realize all the potential conse-quences, or I would have pushed more for regimentation of the blad-der retraining. All I was thinking of was the pain of inserting the straight cath into my urethra and I didn't mind if they missed doing it a time or two).

April 23, 2001

I am so proud. I am breathing on my own, though I still have that piece of tape that covers the trach site so I can talk. When Dr. Hain removed the trach, I had asked, "So what do I do now if I need to be suctioned?" Dr. Hain looks at me and laughs and says "Erika, you cough!" What a simple concept! I had forgotten how and had not had the strength to do so. Not sure I can do it, but I will try. Sounds like it is going to require some serious effort.

Later:

Mom and Ron are in my room. I think it's a Saturday night and we are eating Chinese food. I am weighing in at 88 pounds so anything I might like, I get. They often visit on Saturday nights, bringing food and sometimes even a movie. Mom still has to feed me but that is okay.

All of a sudden, I have to be suctioned, I can't breathe. Mom starts to hit me on the back, she is pulling me over the side of the bed. I cough but it is not hard enough. Finally, I am able to cough and vomit the blockage. These were tough days. I am relearning the basics.

Chapter 7

Setback & Comeback

April 2?, 2001

I have recently started talking about coming home after my sixty days of rehabilitation. Mom is not pleased with this, saying I will require round-the-clock care. Ron is in agreement, go figure; he typically sides with whatever Mom has to say. I think Mom is getting ahead of herself.

I admit that I need to be able to move my hands better than I can currently. But with the help of a special brace, I can brush my teeth and eat a few things with a spoon.

Today I am still not close to self-sufficient and my day starts out at its normal pace. I work with the weekend physical therapist, Jack, and have time only for juice as no one is available to feed me. This means I must take all my meds on an empty stomach. So, I have vomited, which is a fairly normal occurrence. I don't know why I always throw up, but I do. I believe that I am so weak and my stomach is so small, and then we always have problems with that PEG tube converted to the J-tube.

I am still in good spirits when Mom, Ron, Dale, and the kids come bounding through the door at lunchtime. The kids want ice cream, and I'm sure Mom does too as she loves it. They all want to go outside into the courtyard. It is beautiful. I even let Mom take a few photos of me with Jonathan on my lap. This is one of the first times I let anyone take any pictures. I didn't want ANY pictures taken since I fell ill. This is not who I am. I refuse to have it documented.

While outside I am suddenly very cold, and Mom runs to get a blanket. I know this is not going to help, but I want to keep up appearances at least for the kids. Plus, everyone seems happy for the first time in a long time.

Now I am really not feeling well. My teeth start to chatter, I have double vision, and can barely see. They bring me back inside, where Helen, my charge nurse (and a little rough around the edges), ignores my statement that I feel like my throat is closing and I can't breathe. She gives me Ativan and says I am anxious about the trach, stating, "Your throat is supposed to feel that way as it heals from the tracheostomy." But my floater nurse, whoever she is, prevails and takes my temperature. It is 101.8 and she calls the doctor.

The previous day I'd had a different floater; it is hard to get steady help on weekends in the hospital and many things happen. Apparently, the ultrasound scanner wasn't working to see if my bladder was emptying. But I don't believe this had been the only day the scanner wasn't used. The regiment of bladder retraining, as stated in an earlier entry, was not well organized.

Mom and Ron take the kids home. Dale stays. I am really sick and very frightened. We wait for our turn in line for some sort of CT scan or something. Dale is always calm. He tells me he loves me. He holds my hand. It's a different kind of care that he provides. Throughout my illness he has been put down by Mom and Ron for not being able to address the doctors and challenge medical decisions, but he sees *me*, not the illness. Dale calms my spirit. He just wants his wife back.

I don't know the results of that CT scan, but I am admitted to the PCU at Florida Hospital. My admitting diagnosis is threefold: GBS; anemia; and bacteremia with a urinary infection.

April 23, 2001

Mom and Ron come in the morning to see me in the PCU. Mom says I look terrible. I am white as a ghost and my hands are cold.

The nurses last night told me I was "almost septic, a 3+" – whatever that means.

Prior to Mom and Ron's arrival, I am seen by Dr. Feldman, an infectious disease doctor I know from my days at ORMC and Lucerne. Following that visit I see Dr. Masters, my new attending physician. Dr. Masters is still confused as to whether it is sepsis or not. Regardless, they are going to transfer me to another floor.

He mentions that the chest x-ray from the previous night (so that was what Dale and I were waiting for) shows some pneumonia in the lower left lobe. Mom wants to know if it is new; he answers that he hasn't read the report yet. *(I believe this is the doctor that Dale yelled at to stop flirting with the nurses and help his wife. Dale rarely got mad but when he did, watch out!)*

I have also received a couple units of blood, probably to aid with the anemia.

April 24 & April 25, 2001

Mom stays with me in my hospital room. They bring her a cot. My heart rate was up to 150 and my fever is almost 103. Mom is putting iced washcloths on my head, in my groin area and under my arms. It feels like the flu on steroids.

They keep giving me more blood. There are no good answers, I drift in and out of consciousness. I do not recall getting all this blood, nor much else of this time period. *(Good thing Mom has taken some notes.)*

April 26, 2001

Mom goes back to her apartment, where she has been staying because she and Dale cannot get along. I don't understand this. There has been so much drama. When Mom and Ron lived at our house Dale had given up the master bedroom, or rather according to Dale, they took it from him. He says he would have gladly given it up, but he came home one night to find they had moved into our bedroom and moved him out. But what really made him furious was that all my clothes had been boxed up and put under the bed.

(Dale would tell me later that he liked to smell my clothes. It makes him feel as if I am still there, if only for a minute.)

As one can imagine, I am in no position to take sides. I can't imagine that they could not pull it together for the kids and me. But I think people generally think of themselves first. Except my husband. His dad had MS and his mother took care of him until she was well into her 70s. She carried him in and out of the car. Dale can be very selfish, but when it comes to illness he looks at it much differently than others.

April 27, 2001

Mom has gone home, so I am now alone. I am not doing good. I don't know where Dale is. Probably trying to work and deal with the kids. He certainly can't do it all, but I miss him. (He has gone from only working the night shift to doing everything much of the time now. Honestly, taking care of me is a huge job that no one could do. Even with Mom's help it is too much for both of them, I'm sure).

It is the middle of the night and I have been transferred back to the PCU. They want to give me a blood transfusion. I am very confused about what is going on. They say my heart rate has come down to 125. My temperature goes from 101 to 102, always escalating through the night. I call Mom to ask her advice about the blood transfusion. She says, "Erika, you have been receiving blood for days and you need it." I am grateful to hear this. I can tell she is tired but also worried about me. I tell her, "Please don't kill yourself trying to get in here, I will probably be dead before you arrive." This is not to be a sarcastic or manipulative statement; I am surrendering at this point. I truly believed I was not going to make it through the night. I am very tired.

Later:

Dr. Feldman comes to see me. He says I have seven different types of infection in my blood. I have emotionally rallied, and I don't flinch. I look straight at him and say, "So how do we fix this?" He is just as bold and says, "Erika, we knock them out one at a time."

(In Mom's notes, the "infectious disease police" come to my floor, trying to determine where the bacteremia came from. She believes they are trying to "cover their butts.")

Mom has notes of the bacteria found in my blood. So, I have E.coli, along with residuum and several other infections in my blood, as well as several other infections in the urinary tract. Furthermore, I recently had the PICC line removed so Dr. Feldman is not sure if the sepsis is caused by that or the UTIs. I couldn't care less – just fix me.

Dr. Feldman just keeps doing his job, who cares where I got it. He is methodical. His plan is to use antibiotics to kill each individual infection one at a time. He is calm and good at his job. Mom is worried about the fever; Dr. Feldman is not. He says, "It's not the fever that's bothering me, it's what is causing it." Bottom line: I am very sick.

April 28, 2001

I am transferred again, this time to a room next door, I believe I am out of the ICU, yet still in the hospital (not back in the rehab). I remember this room well; it had a lot of windows, and the nurses are kind. They say they will continue to check on me frequently. I feel safer. The urologist wants the urinary catheter taken out (when I was so sick, they had to replace it again). He says he prefers to do sterile intermittent straight cathing.

In addition to this I am again having a lot of problems with my feeding tube. I have to go back to radiology one more time, where they attempt to clean it out. My nurse says many of the medications are getting clogged in the feeding tube. Radiology can unclog it properly (temporarily).

I have been through hell with this feeding tube. If you ever wonder how hard Coca-Cola is on your insides, read on. On mornings the feeding tube was clogged the nurses would pour Coke down it to try to break down the clog. Most days they were successful. Today, however, nothing is working; every quick fix has failed, and it needs real attention. We have been dealing with these temporary fixes and if I can't get my meds we are in trouble. Radiology has to step in.

The scales tip in my favor. They fix the tube.

It looks like I am gonna make it. I am so happy. Mom, however, is furious that I have come this far to nearly die from infections that should and could have been prevented. It truly is unfathomable what I have lived through to nearly be taken out by human error. She is right, but I am out of the woods and that is all I care about.

I look at it differently. So many mistakes have been made. So many unbelievable, horrific events, like the day the nurse closed my door and left me in the chair. I was in pain and couldn't get to the call bell. I sat there for hours. The feeding tube fiasco, the ventilator situation...there are too many to name. The whole experience has left me with a new perspective. I am just grateful to have survived. Although there will be much more and I'm nowhere ready to go home, I'm also not dead (and many thought I would be).

Furthermore, I get to rehab until Jun 9, as I have been in the hospital part of Florida Hospital and the insurance company will subtract the days in the hospital from the 60 days allowed on my plan. Looks like I will be discharged back to rehab and possibly make it home without going to a nursing home.

April 30, 2001

When I first got to Florida Hospital Rehab there was a very young girl, perhaps four or five years of age, who also had Guillain Barre. However, after a few weeks, though still having some struggles, she was well enough to go home.

I can't believe it. Her perfect little four-year-old body and her perfect little four-year-old attitude!! She still has some struggles but is going home. I am both somehow jealous but incredibly happy for her.

I am also thrilled to learn that her room is now available, and I will be moving into the vacant space upon my move back into the rehab part of Florida Hospital! I mean it's not like I can move around or anything but the sun shines in and it's a private room. I feel more at home and most of the staff are getting used to me and happy to see me back.

Even Nurse Betty has become my friend and advocate *(In fact, she will remain my friend for years after I am released from the rehab. Wow, who would have thought?!)*

May 1, 2001

Dale comes and tells me that Mom and Ron had stayed over the previous night and a man tried to get in the house! The man was drunk and confused.

When Mom arrives, she tells me her version. I can't take the tension between them. This is all nuts to me. I want to support my husband and feel somewhat like he is being bullied by Mom and Ron. Let's face it, there is a lot to point out that is negative about Dale, but he is my husband and those are his kids. Yes, I am very grateful for Mom and Ron's help, but this drama doesn't help.

Please stop it.

On a positive note no one can dispute, my son is no longer afraid of me! Dale has brought him in a couple of times during the day when Jessica was in school, and he will sit on my lap.

I am well enough to play peek-a-boo! He laughs and loves it. It makes my heart sing. I miss my kids so much. I can't even imagine what is running through Jessica's young mind. She must feel so abandoned. Dale is not her biological father. She has been late every day to school as Dale can't get up in time and my mom is refusing to pick up the slack, it's like a horrible power play and my daughter is the one hurt.

May 3. 2001

I see myself in the mirror for the first time since I've been ill during physical therapy. This can't be me. I am so skinny. How am I alive? I look like I have been in a concentration camp. I am still trying to stand or at least move my legs.

I am so frustrated with my lack of physical progress. Everything is hard. My arms are coming back but my legs are giving me all sorts of trouble.

They want me to try to walk using a very high walker. I have never seen a walker like this. It's in a triangle shape and fits under my arms trying to hold me up. I cannot do it.

Everyone is rooting for me on the floor, but I get too tired, start to cry, and give up (at least for today).

May 5, 2001

I hop up (to the best of my ability) when I learn a woman is offering to give haircuts in the rehab. It is the first true glimpse of normalcy I have had in months and I am excited.

She comes in to find me waiting in my wheelchair and starts to comb my hair. Thank goodness Mom was there, I would have never been able to explain nor understand what happened to my hair. In fact, this is the first time anyone shows me or tells me what has happened to it.

Remember the haircuts I had made fun of when I first arrived at the rehab? Now I realize that this is exactly what my own hair looks like: short like a pixie in the back with long locks in the front. Their trick to avoid upsetting me while I was at my sickest is now having delayed consequences. I begin to lose it. How dare anyone do this to me? How come no one told me? Mom tries to explain and calm me.

The hairdresser asks if I want to have my hair be even. I give an emphatic NO. I want as much of *me* as used to be there as possible. Let the back grow, pull what you can up into a ponytail.

It is another reminder of how much I have lost and how many things I don't remember. I feel like my life has been stolen from me. So, if nothing else, leave my hair!!!

May 7, 2001

Nurse Betty asks if I want to take an actual shower – something else I haven't had in months. I usually only get sponge baths and they are humiliating, to say the least.

Example: one day the aide sponged me down while talking to her boyfriend, who stood in the hall doing some paperwork or something. I tried to be quiet, I really did, but then it came over me how rude and insensitive she was being. "Look at me," I said, "I'm here, I am a person, and I matter." I then added, "You know, one day this could be you….would you ever want to be treated this way?" When you are paralyzed or in a wheelchair or experiencing some other kind of physical disability you are frequently treated as less than. It is like you have not only lost your ability to ambulate (or whatever); you have lost your brain, and humanity all at the same time.

That girl changed her attitude immediately and apologized. I felt slightly better, knowing she might treat the next person she attended to differently.

Anyway, back to my big move, the shower!! I'm so happy to go in with my Biolage shampoo and so surprised when being moved from the wheelchair to the shower chair hurts. The water hurts, shampooing my hair hurts.

Now to get back to my room, which feels cold. Then they have to brush my hair, which is never gentle. *Hadn't we just used conditioner?*" Sigh. Who would have thought I used to do this every day?

May 8, 2001

I'm weighing in at about 90.2 lbs.!! The gain has come by way of great effort. Every healthcare provider that sees me begs me to eat. Nurses promise to go get me anything I want for dinner or any other time of day.

I do the best I can. I am never hungry. I am often vomiting. But I am getting out of this place if it is the last thing I do.

I remember having days at ORMC when I thought if I could only use my hands or just breathe on my own, I could deal with living in a wheelchair. These days I find that I still have a lot more fight left. I want my whole life back. I want no residual problems. I must be delusional, but I don't care. That is what I want and that is what I'm after.

(Of course, it didn't happen, but I am glad I didn't know that at that time. I remember hearing about a man who completely recovered except for one of his big toes that remained numb and paralyzed. Everyone laughed and thought it was silly that the man might be upset about such a small residual problem, but I didn't think it was funny. That was not going to happen to me. I was getting completely better if I had anything to do with it.)

May 9, 2001

They are late getting me up. I can't exactly dress myself or brush my teeth and I know physical therapy is coming up soon.

For some reason, Cathy Andrews (my doctor friend) and another one of my friends are there. I do not mean to be rude, but it is getting to be that time. I DO NOT miss physical therapy, ever.

Finally, they come in to bathe me and get me ready for therapy. I say, "Forget it, I am going as I am." I can bathe anytime. I need to go to therapy. I am adamant. They all think I am one crazy bitch, but I don't care. I want to recover. No hair-brushing, no teeth-brushing, just take me to therapy.

May 10, 2001

Dale brings the kids in the early evening. He must not have been able to get a sitter. I am still in the physical therapy room. I am practicing standing. I am in a contraption that looks a lot like parallel bars. My legs are aching. Holly is telling me just two more minutes, but then she adds thirty seconds, then another thirty.

Dale is very proud of me. The kids are playing on the balls and other physical therapy paraphernalia. If I had the strength, I would tell them to stop. Holly doesn't seem to mind and laughs at them.

Holly has become a very good friend. She confides in me how her husband had to learn how to live in a wheelchair and he manages at home all day just fine. Apparently, she was his physical therapist. They fell in love and married. I get the sense they have been married for a long time now.

After hearing her story, I feel silly and selfish at times when I complain about being frustrated with not being able to walk.

May 11, 2001

We are starting to go on field trips, designed to get us "disabled misfits" (a term that reflected my feelings of failure at the time) back out in society. This is going to be a disaster, I can feel it. The embarrassment I feel being, or even thinking about being, out in a wheelchair and paralyzed is almost overwhelming.

When I am told I have no choice, I give in and ask where we are going. Nurse Betty reports we are going to "Tar-Jay." I tell her I have never heard of it and she explains that it's just a funny nickname for Target.

And what happens, I ask, if I have to go to the bathroom while we're at Tar-Jay? I am told I will be wearing a diaper. *Wonderful, I can't wait.*

We go, all of us on the short bus. (In reality, it is a van with the word HANDICAPPED in bright red letters on it but in my mind it was definitely the short bus.) They load each of us onto it using that mortifying wheelchair lift – ugh. When will this be over?

I make it, I don't pee myself but must go terribly by the time we return. I do not understand why I have had to experience this. I am not happy.

May 12, 2001

The next outing is the Moorse Museum in Orlando. Though I have never been, I know it's beautiful with many fragile pieces, so why they are bringing a bunch of electric wheelchair-dependent folk (who are really not proficient at maneuvering said wheelchairs) I will never understand. Well, anything is better than Target, so l comply (It's not really a choice, but I feel better thinking I am choosing to go.)

This time we are let off on the street. We are a spectacle to behold. Furthermore, people have the nerve to come up and ask me what happened. *(For some reason they do not seem so interested in the others; perhaps it is my age? Whatever the case, I am getting lots of unwanted attention.)* I cannot believe the audacity of these folks, and sometimes I just turn my head and pretend I don't hear them. Others, I might offer a few words, like, "I am paralyzed."

I'm not trying to be rude, but I can feel their pity (or so it seems) and I hate it.

I am relieved when we finally get inside the museum, however, I am now concerned with navigating the wheelchair, which feels to be roughly the size of a compact car. There are so many knobs and, as mentioned, the coordination in my fingers and hand is not stellar. I am going backward when I want to go forward, turning in circles accidentally far more than anyone would have liked to see. You get the picture.

The museum is beautiful, and I am surprised that I haven't gone before. I am enjoying the beautiful light fixtures and glass pieces, but I'm struggling. Holly has insisted that no one can help me. She wants me to get the hang of this electric wheelchair as it may be as good as it gets for me. I am beyond pissed off as I continually turn in the opposite direction than what's intended, but again, nothing I can do about it. I am at everyone's mercy and this fucking wheelchair is another great sign of it.

I do buy a pretty picture frame for Mom as Mother's Day is coming up and she certainly deserves special appreciation this year.

We are at the end, almost getting back on the special-needs bus, *God help me*! To make matters worse, I must enter the gift shop to get to the exit; yes, the typical marketing trick. Well, the joke was on them. I lose control of the wheelchair and almost take out the entire cashier's stand and a few display items. I make a quick turn and, to everyone's relief, avoid disaster, but I start to cry. I need to go back to the rehab, please.

Later:

We are back, so much for these damn outings. Mom reminds me of a story told by Christopher Reeve (who I admire to no end), about his first try with his electric wheelchair. Apparently, there was a piano being played by an older woman, and he almost took them both out. (In fact, he pushed the piano five feet out with the wheelchair and the pianist never missed a beat!) Lesson learned, never laugh at anyone in an electric wheelchair, for they have mastered a skillset many could not. They are also quite capable of doing a lot of damage, so watch out!

(According to Mom's notes, the hospital staff is down to next to nothing and I keep getting floater nurses who don't know anything of my case. I have to ask for the staff to wash my feeding tube or tell them when an IV has been in too long or to clean my trach. Thank God I can talk now! When you are sick it's very difficult to be your own advocate, but as I learned the hard way, you must try if no one else is around. It is your body! If you have to advocate for yourself, do it!!

One day they didn't cath me at all during the day shift – it had actually been almost twenty-four hours since I had been cathed. I kept saying I needed to be cathed, but they disagreed (hell, they were probably busy). Finally, at my insistence, some nurse did it, and of course 200 cc of urine were expelled. This, despite the fact that the aide in charge of the scanner insisted there was "nothing there." Let's also remember, I had just gotten over the UTI and sepsis, which I had nearly died from, potentially due to a lack of cathing.)

May 13, 2001

It is Mother's Day!! My tribe walks in, except my little Jonathan, who is riding Dale's hip now! Remember before this nightmare he lived on my hip, and I can't help but think I have failed my two beautiful children.

I try to rise above these feelings and focus on the blessings. I focus on their love and the thoughtful gifts they are anxious to give to me. They bring me a book about moms. The kids wrote in it (Jon not as well, but the sentiment was there). Everyone said what a wonderful mom I was, and the book was so special.

Mom got me a new pair of pants and a shirt as I had literally no clothes. But the gift that saved my life was a tape from Christopher Reeve called *Still Me*. It was his story of how he went from being Superman (in the 70s and 80s films, for those too young to remember) to falling off a horse and becoming a quadriplegic. He talks about his feelings. He sounds like me. I relate and listen several times. I force Dale to listen with me (not on Mother's Day of course). Even to me, his story is unimaginable. I am listening and thinking, *Well I can use my hands some and can breathe on my own. I am so much luckier than him. If he can do it, so can I. Thank you, Mom, I really needed to hear his story.*

I give Mom the beautiful glass picture frame from the Moorse Museum, along with the card I'd asked Ron to pick up for me. He also has to write my message as I can't write yet (I do not recall what I dictated to him, but I hope it *was* lovely and that she *felt* my appreciation.)

May 14, 2001

Mom's notes are correct; the staff is limited and abominable. At least I can press the call bell, but this doesn't help much.

I continue to ring the bell because I need my medication, but more importantly, I need to pee.

I wait fifteen minutes, then thirty minutes, and I decide to hit the call bell again (I am now a pro at hitting the call bell these days but I can't get myself to the bathroom). There is no answer or some lame answer when they do pick up. I decide to just pee the bed. Sitting in pee is nothing for me at this point, just relief but boy, having to clean it sure pisses off (pun intended) the aides! I laugh, thinking this is probably one of the first decisions I can make, and actions I can take, to help myself.

May 16, 2001

Well, they have that damn walker out again, the big one. I am not even in the physical therapy room. I am wearing my hospital gown and Holly brings it by and says, "Let's try this again."

All the nurses line up, all the aides, as I WALK using this high walker. Holly says, "Take it easy," and, "Maybe let's turn around," but I want to go all the way to the nurses' station. I make it. All the nurses and aides are clapping and cheering. I did it. Now I need to get back, which is always the hard part. Holly helps me turn the walker.

Tired as hell, I return to my room. I did it! I'm doing it! Holly tells me it is okay to rest now.

May 17, 2001

Jessica makes a singing tape for me. I start crying as I listen to her sweet voice. (I don't remember the song itself and unfortunately I don't have the tape, so I have to rely on Mom's notes. Honestly, some of these memories are so painful I have to reach hard into the echoes of my mind to retrieve them. I shoved them way down so I could stay focused and survive, so I am incredibly grateful to Mom for keeping this record.)

I miss my daughter so much. I should be home playing checkers with her. I had bought her a cute little laptop to play with for Christmas (she loved it and wanted me to spend a lot of time playing it with her. How I wished I had, but I was always busy. Busy means nothing now).

(It has been a relentless battle to forgive myself for getting sick. There is no one to blame, but it did a lot of damage to both my

children and was a huge loss for me as well. I had to go into a zone in order to live. I couldn't spend too much time thinking about how my daughter felt. I would have died. I could not think of anything but, "Fight Erika, get out of here – live." I look back and it brings up so much pain, but I don't think I had any other energy at the time. Since then, I reflect often on how this affected each child differently. I reflect on how grateful I should have been to Dale but still found fault with him once out of the hospital (mind you, fault was there, but isn't it always?). I wish I had told my mother "Thank you" more often, and I now say to anyone who will listen how Ron Wohlwend saved my life by insisting that I have the dangerous lung surgery. I just don't know if I said it to him enough. I hope he knows. I hope Mom is looking over my shoulder as I am writing this, finally, almost six months after she passed.)

Jessica was singing, "I'm thinking about you, I wish you were home. Mom, just come home. We hope you come home soon." According to Mom, Jessica has dealt with my absence, now over four months, extremely well. She also believes, however, that Jessica keeps a lot of her feelings to herself. But I already know this. I know my daughter well. Since her birth I have been Jessica's rock, the one person she could count on, and now I am not there.

I know Jessica would tell me her feelings if I were home, but I am not. My girl. My heart breaks again as I write this.

May 18, 2001

Mom is pushing for me to go to a nursing home after my rehab days are up. She is visiting all of them. She is telling me all the great things about them. I am not sold. Dale is not sold. He says he will carry me up and down the stairs each day as her big concern is there is no downstairs shower in our home. Dr. Creamer agrees with Dale and is in disbelief that a nursing home is even an option. One day he came to my room alone to tell me he had many quadriplegics go home, as long as they have help. He said it in such a way that didn't discount or put my mother down but helped me think that it certainly could be done. I really appreciate him. He goes the extra mile, like so many of the doctors did. Not all, but a lot did, and it made a difference. Doctors, don't think we don't remember you. We do. For many of us you are a game-changer.

Mom and the case management team (Mom had way too much power here) come up with a plan for me to return home. *I love my mother and know she did what she could, but this should have been Dale. I look back and see how much he was left out. He was who I lived with and should have had more input. Mom was brilliant, don't get me wrong but I wanted my life back and she wanted to be in a position where she didn't have to worry anymore. Dale wanted his wife home, no matter what that looked like. I could see both sides.)*

Anyway, the treatment plan (or list of achievements I needed to make) in order to go home is ridiculous. It was like asking me to swim the English Channel. I was barely walking, and they said I had to do steps, feed myself without that apparatus (the glove with forks and spoons, et cetera), along with many other boxes to check. Of course, my biggest concern was the steps. We all knew it.

I start thinking out of the box, like moving to a one-story home. What a novel idea, something that might work. I had a visit from another woman who had GBS (*Once you have had it you are more than welcome to become a volunteer to talk to those who have it, and most of us do*).

Trudy, the woman who visits, had GBS three years ago and struggles with steps. I ask what she does, she says she just doesn't use steps. Well, that is easy enough.

Dale is on board, but we have a lot of pushback from case management.

At this time, Mom has an attorney write up a post-nuptial agreement between me and Dale. As mentioned, Dale has a lot of problems with money. He owes child support for his kids from a previous marriage; he also owes the IRS and many others as well. I keep finding out about more and more debt. He is a great man but has struggled with managing his money. Debts prior to our marriage are not always things I am aware of and I think he thought he could fix them without pulling me into the mix. Mom wants to help me separate our finances so that at least one of us could have assets in their name. That one would be me. I had assets. We needed to protect them. What would we do if the IRS took our house? *(Seems silly now as the IRS couldn't get our house but there were a lot of unknowns and lots more to worry about. Mom was trying to protect us. Dale agrees.)*

I always feel bad for doing this to Dale, yet I didn't know any other solution. There must have been another solution, but we had so much going on.

May 20, 2001

More drama at the house. How can this all be?

Dale wants to go see his son, who as mentioned was from a previous marriage, graduate from eighth grade. *(Again, my memory is fuzzy here. According to Mom's notes he wanted to go for seven days. I remember three days. Regardless, Mom says she won't take care of the kids and he should not leave me. I laugh as I write this, Mom took a few breaks, I guess she figures she wasn't married to me. Mom goes with Ron to Chicago for four days. The situation is bringing out the worst in everyone – it is as simple as that.)*

I am not sure what is happening at that house and honestly I don't even want to know. I feel bad for Dale, but I also feel hurt that he would want to leave me. This is completely irrational, but I am still very needy. I need a break too!!

I am getting very depressed. I ask for antidepressants. I don't know if I take them or not, because I am still taking so many pills.

May 22, 2001

I can paint!! This is our activity in recreational therapy. I never could paint well so my ability has not changed all that much. I paint a pretty box in the shape of a heart. I try to put flowers on the top.

I am very proud of my painting and leave it out for years after my release from the hospital. In fact, it still resides somewhere in my house.

I can now participate in the recreational hour and don't think it is so stupid anymore. Funny how my perspective has changed.

May 28, 2001

It is my thirty-eighth birthday!! Mom has planned a surprise party for me. I can use a regular walker now to get to the rec room on the floor. I even put on my makeup. Lipstick is always tried, though not always successful. Occasionally I can get a nurse to do mascara, et cetera.

When I walk into the recreation room, I find it decorated with balloons and a cake. Jessica puts on a gymnastics show. A lot of people are there, some of whom I don't know. Most, besides my family, are residents of the rehab. One gentleman stays all day. He may have been a stroke victim, but he just stayed and watched. Strange how we find joy in just about anything positive when we are brought to our knees.

It is a joyous day with many pictures taken. I can see on Ron's awestruck face that he is giving many thanks to God. Ron is very Catholic and has a strong connection to his faith, he has prayed fervently throughout this entire journey. I am so grateful. If I ever doubted Jesus, that ended with this illness, for I saw Him many times during my bad days and knew He was with me. There is no denying it. If you are not a Christian, it doesn't matter. There is a force stronger than all of us. I've seen it.

May 29, 2001

Mom has made Dale look at some of the nursing homes. He is adamantly opposed to the idea.

Dale doesn't get to see his son graduate. Dale has sacrificed a lot. He needs to be recognized. Thank you, Dale, for all you have done. *(I don't think I formally thanked him— or at least not enough – and in writing this I am brought to tears at all the sacrificing he did with no complaint, no "I need some me time", nothing. He was just there. One day, months out of the hospital, Dale sat in my wheelchair and said, "I am exhausted. I need one of these." That was about all the complaining he did.)*

Mom has sacrificed also and been a wonderful medical advocate, but I know she is cooked now. There really is no reason I can't go home, and she knows it. She somehow thinks she will have to be with me twenty-four hours a day. Everyone is different - my neighbor at the rehab with the brain bleed is going home. He cannot walk or talk but his mom wants him home and she is willing to take care of him.

My mom has really stepped up for me over the last five months, but that is not the type of mom she is so it has been especially hard for her. My mother very much has her own life – she loves to travel and is a successful realtor – and I recognize that. I am grateful and I know she wants to go home and has had enough, and it makes me feel terrible. Knowing someone's limitations and being able to live with them is so incredibly hard.

Every time someone gets up and walks out of the room, I am reminded that I can't do that. I can't do what they call ADLs (activities of daily living). *(I know it's hard to be a caregiver, but they must also be aware that the patient has no choice and has a different perspective. I now specialize in helping those with physical ailments as a licensed mental health counselor. I always want to speak with the whole family but the whole family rarely wants to speak. If you love someone who is ill, acutely or chronically, you are part of a system, like it or not. And always remember that while you can walk away and take your "me time," they can't. They depend on you and usually hate it. No one wants to be a bother. But this is all for another book, another day, from another perspective.)*

June 2, 2001

Today is Jonathan's graduation from Living Word Academy, where he goes to preschool and we go to church. He is two, not sure what he is graduating from, but after much coordination, I'm going to be there.

Somehow, I get there. I walk in with my walker (and my leg braces of course) and have a steadier gait. I am up to a hundred pounds and my face has filled out. *(Mom wrote in her notes that I looked absolutely beautiful, and anyone who had seen me a month earlier wouldn't have believed I was the same person.)*

I cry a lot during the ceremony. When Jonathan gets his diploma, the school director points out that I am there, calling it a miracle. And it is! After all the hoopla, Dale takes me back to the rehab in a wheelchair. I am so tired, but I want him to stay but of course he can't.

June 3, 2001

In the rehab we have a set of five steps with a chair at the top to rest (unfortunately you then have to go down them as well). For the longest time I was terrified of those steps, but people have made it a condition of my going home. I tell Holly I am ready to try and pray that God is with me. I wind up walking up the steps two different times! I feel like I am the queen of the world. I am amazed… only a week ago I couldn't make one step. I am being carried and I know it. No stopping me now.

I call Mom. I am so excited. So it's not perfect, I have to use a cane and a harness, but I did it! I think I can come home. Mom is not so sure. She reminds me that it is a full flight of steps at home and that I am still being straight cathed several times a day, not to mention that I still have a feeding tube.

This doesn't dampen my excitement. I had set a goal of being able to walk with a walker within a year of going to rehab, and I am already doing that now!

Mom is still looking into nursing homes. She is also laying down the law about how much she will help if I don't go to one: two and a half days a week. That's her limit.

The woman is burnt out. I can feel it, and it doesn't feel good.

June 6. 2001

Today will determine if I go home or to a nursing home. As we know, Mom has been trying to convince me to go to the nursing home, and so has some of the staff. Today I have to prove to them all what I can do.

For starters, I do the five stairs that have been demanded of me (the rehab steps). Mom says, "Well, that is great, but you have a full set of stairs at home." The case manager's ears perk up and she says, "We have a full set of stairs in the hall. Try that, Erika."

I'm nervous as hell but I walk to the stairs and grab hold of that railing. I do it! Now I must walk down. I do this too. This is an act that God graced upon me this day, I know it. Days before I couldn't have done the five stairs.

So now everyone had to shut up about the stair situation. I seemed to be doing better with the catheter situation so straight cathing is no longer an issue.

The feeding tube has also been removed.

June 7, 2001

I am so excited to speak to Mom when she comes into my room. I have so much to tell her! I had been sitting with the social worker who said my insurance would pay for physical and occupational therapy at home.

Mom is so pro-nursing home. I still can't figure it out, but I think it gives her a feeling of safety for me. The little apartment she rented when she moved out of my house is right across the street from the nursing home she is advocating for, *but do I need a nursing home?* I have been in the hospital/rehab for nearly six months. I can walk with a walker and I can do stairs; I am skinny and weak, but why can't I go home?

I do think she is ready to regain her own life. I am ready to regain mine. I still have a long way to go but don't hold me back out of your fear. It's okay if you can't help, Mom. I know she feels this duty but on the receiving end it doesn't feel so great. I don't want to be anyone's duty.

(As I read through Momma's notes, she does give me a lot of "atta girls." She notes my determination and dedication. She wonders if it came from all those years as a competitive swimmer. Nothing ever held me back. One year, when I had a broken arm, I taped it with a plastic bag and kicked in the mornings with the boys' high school swim team. I was eleven years old!)

I have already gone home for a few trial runs, and I hated how it looked. I like it all a certain way. I want normal. A test run home is not so normal.

I will be going home, though. That is what is important to me. I will be wearing my leg braces and probably be in my wheelchair; I will also have a walker, two canes, a shower chair, a potty chair, and a urinary tract infection.

June 8, 2001

This is the day I come home!! I have been hospitalized for nearly six months. They have packed me up and Holly (my physical therapist) is tying my shoes. I am crying and asking, "Can I do this? I feel like I have failed as I cannot walk on my own. I remember telling Holly how jealous I was of the young man who had the brain bleed as he was able to master walking before me. I remember her classic response: "Erika, he has brain damage, do you really hear yourself?" She was always good at putting things in perspective. She whispers in my ear as I am ready to leave, "Erika, it's going to be okay, take it a day at a time." I am disappointed because I want her to promise me that I will walk again. I am so grateful God put her in my life at that point. She is gentle and strong and knows when to use each of those traits.

I ask Mom to take the kids overnight so I can settle in and surprise them in the morning. Going home is going to be enough for me. If nothing else, I still have the stairs to contend with at home *(it will all prove harder than I ever imagined.)*

Dale comes to get me, and on the way home there is an accident on Rt. 4 in Orlando. We are going absolutely nowhere fast, and Dale is irritated. We are in his truck because I had so much stuff to bring home with me, which means we have no air conditioning. Remember it's Florida in June, so it's hot. But I couldn't care less; I am free.

Finally, we get home. It is late and I'm tired, but I am also extremely happy! Dale follows me up the stairs, but I am able to do them myself!! I'm so excited! I ask Dale if he will help me with a shower. Unfortunately, he has to hold me up to move me into the shower chair. I am scared. I know this is hard for him and I am screaming in pain. My whole body still hurts, especially my feet. He says he's got me. He does, but I am upset that I need that much help. Thank God he is not that upset. He sets up the porta-potty by the bed in case I need to go so I don't have to put the braces on. I think I can transfer from the bed to the porta-potty by myself. *(I cannot do this task either and end up asking him for help.)*

The hardest part comes when we go to bed. I want my husband to get in bed and hold me. I want to be his wife again not just his patient. Unfortunately, any real touch still hurts too much. I cry. He says it will pass. He kisses me and I spend my first night back in my own bed.

June 9, 2001

Dale gets up and empties the porta-potty. Who does this for someone?? It's an unimaginable kindness, but there is no time to dwell. The kids will be here soon.

I realize I don't have the strength to press the antiperspirant. I am discouraged but Dale gladly helps.

Okay – we are ready. Jessica has been praying that I am moved to the nursing home near Hunters Creek where we live so she will be very surprised.

The door opens, I am sitting on my green couch that reclines. Both kids run to me. They throw themselves on top of me. Tears fall from all of us. Jessica just keeps repeating "You're home forever now?" She can't believe it. I can't believe it. And I question, am I well enough to be their mom?

But for today, this is a victory. I play with Jessica on her laptop. I have a hard time pressing buttons, but she helps.

Chapter 3

A New Life

So, I am home. What next? Not a dull moment.

Mom is staying at the house to help the first few days, and Jessica's dance recital is imminent.

(I remember the recital, but I also remember Jessica couldn't find me after the show because I couldn't go upstairs to help her get undressed. Bittersweet.)

Every day I try. I have physical therapy at the house. I try to show off for Dale and the kids every breakfast. I try to make it across the kitchen with the canes. I am tired of the walker. So, the first day it is two canes, one cane, then I scurry across with no canes, only my leg braces.

I improve quickly. My home physical therapist says I need to go to CORA Rehabilitation Outpatient because I have surpassed all she has to offer. Mom stays some days but sits in the other room. She is burnt out and depressed. She won't even watch TV with me. I know she wants her life back. We get into it and she goes. She needs to go. She has done more than she had been capable of doing and probably more than anyone could expect.

As being left alone will not work for me, we hired Granny Nannies until I can drive and do more of my daily activities unaided. *(Boy, I hated them. They probably hated me too. I was not an easy client.)*

Less than a month out of the hospital Jonathan's birthday is quickly approaching. I want to make it especially over the top. So many people to thank, so much to be grateful for, I have to make it big. Jonathan loves Elmo, so I invite him. Then I invite everyone we know, everyone who has been so helpful.

(I did not want anyone to know how much I struggled so I removed all the potty chairs that raised the toilet seat to a level that made it easier for me to get up and down. I got rid of any sign of sickness. The only thing I couldn't get rid of was the damn leg braces. I had no dorsiflexion, meaning I had terrible foot drop and my feet were totally paralyzed – not to mention that the nerve damage left me feeling like a thousand knives were being poked in my feet and up my legs all day. It was even worse at night.)

The party is a smash except that Jonathan is terrified of Elmo! Some folks comment that they would have never known I had been sick except for the leg braces. I pretty much just sit in the corner and talk. I think everyone understands that even that took a lot of energy.

Granny Nannies fire me. They say I was difficult. *I was difficult.* I want my life back. I have Dale teach me how to drive again. I don't have normal sensation in my feet, so this is hard. I also can't turn my head to look behind me. *(I don't know why that was.)* I then retake the driver's test to make sure I am safe, and the only comment is that I didn't look behind me as I backed up. (The instructor didn't need to know this is because I couldn't, so I didn't tell him. Eventually, it did go away. It would be years before some of this improved, but eventually it did.)

I go to CORA Rehabilitation Center, and when I speak of Jessica and Jonathan, the therapist asks if they are my grandkids. I am thirty-eight. I was beautiful; now I am very skinny and apparently look old. I'm also trying to get my hair to all one length. I go to CORA almost every day for years. When the insurance stops paying, I pay myself

I go for my first haircut outside of rehab. Explaining the earlier haircut was too much to get into (let alone in the hairdresser's chair), so I say, "Just try to even it up." It was short for me, but I begin accepting what is. The fragmented parts of me needed to come together: I was trying, along with everyone else who loved me, and was living this new life.

I am doing it. I pick Jonathan up early many days so we can nap together, except that he doesn't nap.

I am cooking for my family again. It's slow but life is coming together. I tell Dale we must go on vacation. He looks at me cross-eyed. I say, "Just to the beach," and we go. We go a couple of times. The first time was a disaster. My shower chair wouldn't fit in the shower, and I cried and cried.

The next time I was somewhat better, I think we were in Daytona Beach. Yes, the beach where cars can be on it, and you had better be on top of your kids or they are gonna get killed. One lady yelled at me because I didn't have a handle on Jonathan like I should have. I couldn't. Jessica helped a lot in those days. Especially early on, Jon knew he could outrun me and usually did. Jessica would grab him for me.

Anyway, back to Daytona Beach, my real recovery. We are acting normal, within limits. I ask Dale if he is embarrassed to be with me in a wheelchair and leg braces. He reluctantly admits that sometimes he is a little embarrassed as I am so young, and folks look at us.

So of course, that night at dinner I give him a good reaming out - "How dare you say that" et cetera – but the next morning I take off those damn leg braces. I am literally falling into walls. I think Dale had taken the kids to the pool or something. Everyone kept asking if they could help me. I said no. I was gonna get this.

I really was struggling, and I don't know how long it took me to be able to gain some balance and walk with my paralyzed feet that hurt continuously. But I did it!

In the fall, Jessica started second grade and I went to her school. It was gym time and we had to walk to the field in the back of the school. I was so far behind everyone. Jessica and her friend stayed with me. Jess's friend said, "It's okay, I have an uncle that walks real slow too, we will get there." Jessica just hung in with Mom.

I still see Dr. Creamer from the rehab for pain management and direction. I was introduced to Dr. Gary Weiss, who still is my doctor today. He has always listened to me. Some of my illnesses have been very rare but he always knew that if I said something was wrong, something was wrong, and he has always stuck by me. Again, a book for another day.

Beyond blessed. I couldn't return to work but needed some purpose and decided I wanted to get my master's in counseling psychology and help the folks in need, just like the John fellow I hated at the rehab. So, I did. It took forever because I kept getting sick but that is for another book.

After a couple of years of total devotion to rehab, I finally returned to my job at Darden Restaurants as a software engineer. Life went back to normal. There were lots of late-night snacks with Jonathan to gain weight. Jessica just wanted me to be able to ride a roller coaster. I cried because when she asked this I didn't know if I'd ever walk. Jessica and I have ridden many roller coasters, literally and figuratively, since then, as have both Jonathan and Dale. It's been a wild ride.

I have tried to give back when I haven't been ill. I hope this book in some way helps someone who feels they have been handed too much to bear.

It has helped me. It only took twenty-plus years to write. Some of the memories were way too painful. It's out now.

My perspective is forever changed. Any day off a ventilator is a good day.

I remember laying in the hospital bed and realizing it is not work that matters, it's the loving memories and relationships. I also remember thinking that I had never eaten dinner in my dining room as I wanted to save it for special occasions. While I am still a little nutty about the white furniture, I love to eat in the dining room now. Love on your people. Never judge as we never know.

I brought my kids to nursing homes many times when they were small. I volunteered for the sick and still do. Many folks thought it was awful that I brought my small children to nursing homes (we did have a dear friend in a nursing home from Guillain-Barre who hadn't recovered enough). My thought was always to teach my kids that health is a gift not given to everyone, and to be grateful and help others.

As mentioned, my dear mother is not here to read this. She passed on February 10, 2022. I got to be her caretaker. It was probably all part of a greater plan. As mentioned throughout, Mom's journal was especially helpful in writing this. I had some memories – in fact, a lot of memories – but dates and specifics I got from her notes. So, many thanks to Mom in heaven. Sad she is not here to read this, as she gave me the journal to start writing in so many years ago. Mom was big on journaling.

In Mom's journal, she closes with this quote:

"A hero is an ordinary individual who finds the strength to persevere in spite of overwhelming obstacles; a fifteen-year-old boy who landed on his head while wrestling with his brother, leaving him barely able to swallow or speak: Travis Roy, paralyzed the first thirty seconds of a hockey game in his freshman year at college. These are the real heroes and so are the families and friends who have stood by them."

Mom added to this…

"And I feel that Erika Orriss' name belongs in the above quote as she has found the strength to persevere despite her overwhelming obstacles. When illness, tragedy, et cetera comes to anyone who reads this journal (as it eventually will), May we remember Erika's courage and hope that we can measure up in even a small way to Erika, a true hero."

Boy, that is a lot to live up to…but I will. I will make every day count.

Blessings,

Erika Orriss

.

Acknowledgments
(there are many)

*M*y children Jessica and Jonathan whom I fought for throughout the illness, I refused to let them grow up without a mother. They were my main incentive of which made me push forward every day even on days I wanted to give up.

My husband, Dale Orriss, who was able to stay as calm as a cucumber (or appeared that way) and brought peace to me throughout an otherwise anxiety-ridden journey. He remained steadfast, faithful, and always believed I would recover.

My mother, who stepped in and took action. She was a superhero dealing with the medical staff, braiding my hair, and insurance issues. She was invaluable in my care and support.

Her husband, Ron Wohlwend, who supported me in many ways. He also was a great support to my mother who desperately needed it.

My Aunt Carol, who when asked via lip reading if I would live (this is when the doctors were telling me I was going to die and to get my financial affairs in order). She said emphatically, "NO." This was paramount as I believed her, and I think this made a huge difference in my recovery.

My Aunt Priscilla, who supported my mother and me and came to visit. She is a nurse and was able to offer advice during difficult times. I remember her telling me she loved me.

My cousin Carolyn, who fought for a J-tube when they could not get the peg tube to work.

All my extended family, who sent letters, gifts, and uplifted my spirits.

My dear friends, who did things like brushed my teeth, cut my hair, and put makeup on me so I felt somewhat human.

Our neighbors, who watched the kids at night so Dale could come and see me when my mother was not available to watch them.

All the staff at Orlando Regional Medical Center including but not limited to Staff clergy, who prayed with me.

ICU Nurse Dan
Dr. Darrin Wolffe, my primary doctor, who called all the shots.
Dr. Gregory, who performed the lung surgery.
Dr. Commadore, who recognized the symptoms of Guillain-Barre Syndrome.
Dr. Bass, my pulmonologist, who later let me do a swallow study with a Coca-Cola and it worked.

All the staff at Florida Hospital Rehabilitation Center, including but not limited to:

Nurse Betty and her team, who tried to help when even short-staffed.

Holly, my physical therapist at Florida Hospital Rehab. She performed miracles.

Dr Hain, my pulmonologist at Florida Hospital Rehab, who ultimately took out the trach.

John, my social worker. I never gave him enough credit.

Dr. Feldman, my infectious disease specialist, without whom I am sure I would not be alive.

Dr. Creamer, who encouraged me to return home rather than go to a nursing home despite my family's fears. His final talk with me gave me such hope to continue on with life, no matter what that looked like. He managed my pain for a long time afterward.

The CORA Rehabilitation Center in Orlando Florida, which allowed me to receive care well after my allotted insurance regulations had run out. (I did pay out of pocket but they never gave up and were a steady in my recovery.)

I must recognize my current neurologist, Dr. Gary Weiss, whom I started seeing about six months after my release from the hospital and has been a constant source of information and support for more than twenty years.

I am sure I owe a debt of gratitude to so many more that I could not possibly list everyone by name. However, you know who you are and are held dearly in my heart. I will never forget the kindnesses you bestowed upon me.

Thank you.

About the Author

*E*rika L. Orriss lives in Satellite Beach Florida, about an hour east of the hospital that saved her life. She moved over for a business opportunity and stayed for the ocean. She enjoys any water-related activity. She is active politically, socially, and environmentally within her community

Erika stopped working in software when another autoimmune illness hit a flare and her primary neurologist said, "You have this master's degree and a lot of history to help others – use it. It will allow you to have a more flexible schedule and still give back which has been your focus all along." Her doctors never thought she would go back to work, but she did and except for brief periods of disability absence, she had almost thirty years in the corporate world as a successful software engineer.

She currently manages her own hours working as a licensed mental health counselor in Melbourne, Florida. She specializes in helping those suffering from chronic illness, mental and otherwise.

Erika loves to do yoga, although her feet never really came back and she sometimes falls over. She remains open to try just about anything once. She does not think of herself as disabled, but her body at times reminds her. She plays drums, has a dog, loves to kayak, and raise awareness for rare diseases.

Erika and Dale Orriss are no longer married but remain very close. Her children rebounded well from a challenging upbringing. Her daughter Jessica is married and holds a graduate degree in Engineering from Georgia Tech, and "baby" Jonathan is graduating from Florida State University with a degree in Economics.

Her family remains very close from ties that bind beyond human understanding. Erika was given the opportunity to help take care of her mother before her passing in February 2022.

Erika is looking to complete a doctoral program to better understand neurological/neuromuscular disorders and considering running for public office.

Taking Action

When I was diagnosed with Guillain-Barre Syndrome I had no idea what it was. No one had heard of it before. I was lucky enough to have a neurologist who had just had it himself. A disease is considered rare if it affects only 5-6% of the population and is usually chronic and or genetic. Fewer than 20,000 will present with Guillain-Barre Syndrome annually.

So, just what is Guillain-Barre (GBS)? Guillain-Barré (pronounced Ghee-yan Bah-ray) Syndrome is an inflammatory disorder of the peripheral nerves outside the brain and spinal cord. It's also called Acute Inflammatory Demyelinating Polyneuropathy or Landry's Ascending Paralysis.

GBS is characterized by the rapid onset of *numbness, weakness,* and often *paralysis* of the legs, arms, breathing muscles, and face. Paralysis is *ascending*, meaning that it travels up the limbs from fingers and toes toward the torso. Loss of reflexes, such as the knee jerk, is usually found.

The cause of GBS is unknown. We do know that about 50% of cases occur shortly after a microbial infection (viral or bacterial), some as simple and common as the flu or food poisoning. Some theories suggest an autoimmune trigger, in which the patient's defense system of antibodies and white blood cells are called into action against the body, damaging myelin (nerve covering or insulation), leading to numbness and weakness.

As GBS is potentially life-threatening, most newly diagnosed patients are hospitalized. GBS is very unpredictable in its early stages, so it is treated conservatively. Usually, a new case of GBS is admitted to ICU (Intensive Care) to monitor breathing and other body functions until the disease is stabilized. Plasma exchange (a blood "cleansing" procedure) and high-dose intravenous immune globulins are often helpful to shorten the course of GBS. The acute phase of GBS typically varies in length from a few days to months, with over 90% of patients moving into the rehabilitative phase within four weeks. Patient care involves the coordinated efforts of a team such as a neurologist, physiatrist (rehabilitation physician), internist, family physician, physical therapist, occupational therapist, social worker, nurse, and psychologist or psychiatrist. Some patients require speech therapy if their speech muscles have been affected.

There are many variants of GBS but they all share the characteristic of being "rapid onset." Variants exist of Acute Inflammatory Demyelinating Polyneuropathy (AIDP), although 75% – 80% of cases fall into this "classic" category. These variants include:

- Acute Motor Axonal Neuropathy (AMAN) (similar to AIDP but without sensory symptoms)
- Acute Motor Sensory Axonal Neuropathy (AMSAN) (a severe variant of GBS more prevalent in Asia, Central America, and South America)
- Miller Fisher Syndrome (characterized by double vision, loss of balance, and deep tendon reflexes)

Recovery from GBS may occur over six months to two years or longer. A particularly frustrating consequence of GBS is long-term recurrences of fatigue and/or exhaustion as well as abnormal sensations including pain and muscle aches. I was afraid to drive for years after GBS as many times I started to fall asleep. This issue did resolve but my feet continue to suffer from severe neuropathy, along with abnormal sensations. My hands seem to have the same issue but to a lesser extent. For most of us, these annoyances can be aggravated by "normal" activity and can be alleviated by pacing activity and rest.

Further literature claims the majority of people with GBS recover completely or nearly completely; however, some have mild residual effects such as foot drop or abnormal feeling in the feet and hands for two years or more. Persistent fatigue and pain may remain problematic (as in my case). It is also said that fewer than 15 percent have substantial long-term disability severe enough to need a cane, walker or wheelchair; however, I have met many of them. Perhaps this is due to the circles I run in. Death from GBS does occur, but in fewer than 5 percent of patients and is rare in countries with intensive care facilities, although I was expected to die for much of my ICU stay. Finally, though the data indicates that recurrence is rare, I met a few individuals who had it more than once, including one woman who had it three times.

This book only addresses Guillain-Barre because it is based on my experience; however, there are many rare disorders. The FDA claims there are over 7 million such diseases affecting more than 30 million people in the United States. Diagnosing rare diseases is incredibly difficult as individuals with the same disease often present with different symptoms. The diagnostic delay for rare diseases can be from months to decades, depending on the individual's phenotype, age, and resources. The average time for a rare disease to be diagnosed appears to be 4-5 years; however, in some cases it can take over a decade.

Most rare diseases are life-threatening and have no treatment. Also keep in mind that there are other rare diseases that have not been identified; nor is there adequate funding for research to be done on them. As a result, many suffer in silence and may remain undiagnosed or even misdiagnosed, which further adds emotional distress for them and their family members. These folks are often told they are crazy or that they have some sort of mental disorder. This is particularly true for women.

Long after my Guillain-Barre days, I ran into a great organization called the National Organization of Rare Disorders (NORD). They were and have been an incredibly helpful resource. Every year they hold National Rare Disease Day, which is the last day in February. (It may fall on February 29 on leap years. This is to signify the rarity of each illness.)

The mascot for NORD is a zebra; this is because as doctors are going through medical school they are told, "When you hear hoof beats, look for horses, not zebras." But there are zebras and although fewer in number their pain needs to be addressed.

I would be remiss if I didn't mention the GBS Society. They are a very supportive foundation for the patient and the family. My daughter even wrote an article when she was about nine years old that was published in the GBS newsletter. They provided much-needed information. They also provided an online support group that I found immensely helpful during my initial months after returning home. I cannot thank them enough. Additionally, they hold conferences that allow patients to share their experiences and health care professionals to give the latest and greatest information on Guillain-Barre Syndrome.

As of today, we still have no direct correlation or cure. Many receive IVIG or plasmapheresis to stop the attack on the body, but they don't always work. This was true in my case, though I received a dangerous number of rounds of each. Years later I went back for plasmapheresis for another autoimmune illness and met the man who had helped me years before. I said, "Oh, I got so many rounds of this when I had Guillain-Barre and it didn't work." He looked at me and said, "Well, one might argue that you wouldn't be here without it." I am certainly glad they tried everything they could.

Please visit the websites of both organizations and consider taking action or giving financially. The stories will touch your heart.

Home - GBS/CIDP Foundation International (gbs-cidp.org) – you can donate or look into the advocacy page.

Home - NORD (National Organization for Rare Disorders) (rarediseases.org)

Captured Moments

Picture of the kids and I the Christmas prior, beginning to not feel well.

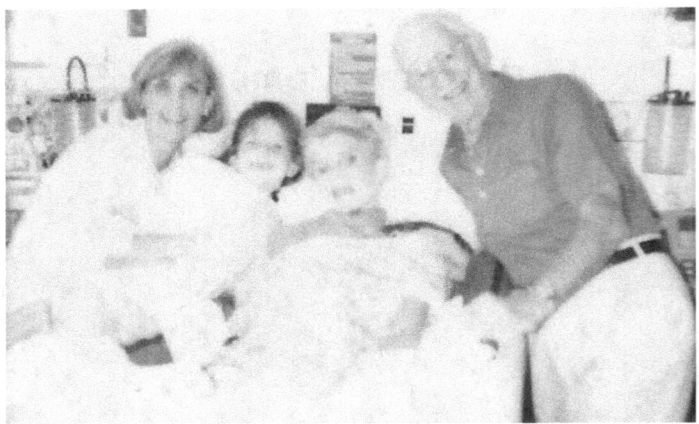

The first time I saw my children after admission to the hospital. It had been six weeks. Picture shows Mom, Jessica, myself and Ron. We had carefully tried to hide all the tubes from the tracheostomy to the catheter. Jonathan got frightened and Dale had to take him outside.

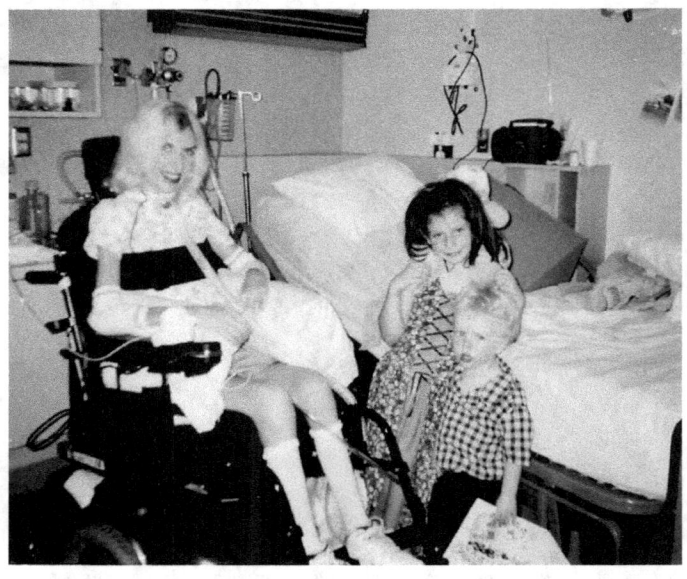

Easter 2001. It was a good day. The pillows and wraps on my arms were to protect my skin. I was so thin and already had a bedsore. They were trying to keep me from getting any more.

A rare day at Florida Rehabilitation Center courtyard with my children. This is one of the few photos I allowed. I was still on the trach collar. I would eventually go inside as this was the beginning of sepsis and I was not feeling well.

Jonathan's graduation from his preschool class. Shown: Jessica, dear friend from church who often watched the kids for Dale, myself, Dale, and Jonathan

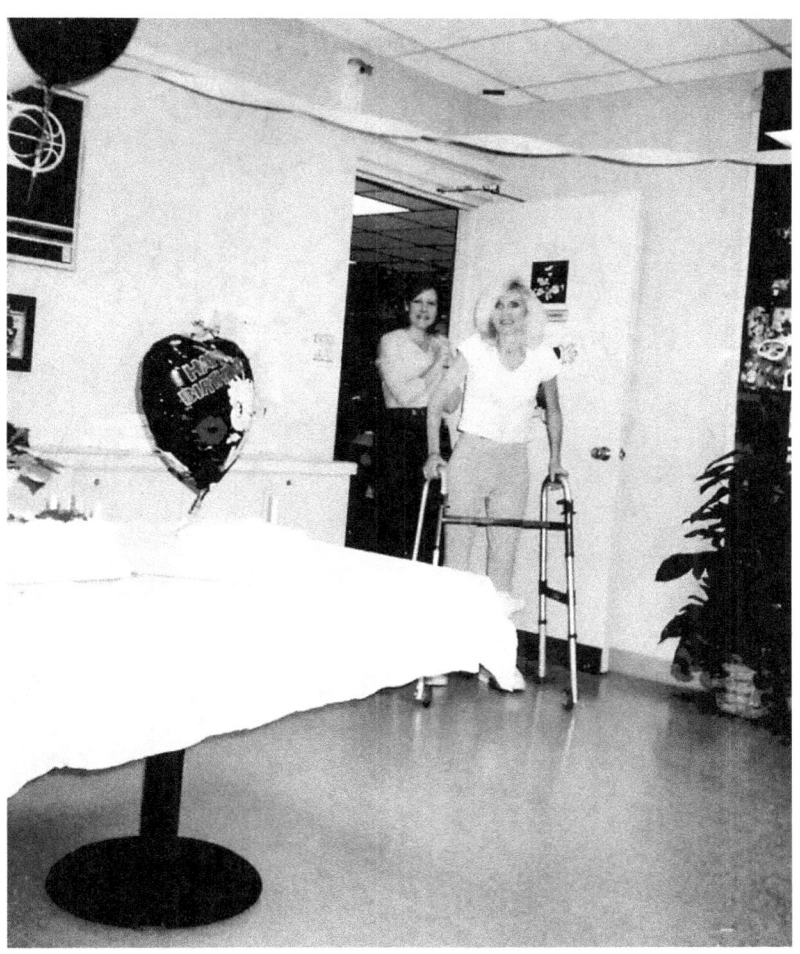

Myself walking into my surprise 38th birthday party.
It was May 28th.

Myself and my beautiful children at my birthday party.
The fellow included in the picture stayed all day.
He was another resident at the rehab.

Ron, myself, and mom at my birthday party

To: Lowenstein Christina
From: Barbara Wohlwend <barb@strato.net>
Subject: Email from Erika (dictated to Barbara on 4/3/01)
Cc:
Bcc:
X-Attachments:

To the Healy Family and All In-Laws,

Lord knows there are a lot you! I couldn't respond to all the
letters, gifts, and especially the love that I've received from you
all. But they are all heartfelt and have brought me great joy in
knowing that you are thinking about me.

It was wonderful to see you all at Thanksgiving. I was so glad I got
that opportunity because shortly thereafter, as you know, I got sick.

It's been a long, slow process in recovery, but I can now talk, move
my arms, and eat. Recovery from this virus is very slow, but at least
it looks like there is recovery. So right now I am in Florida
Hospital Rehab, where they are working me out 46 hrs. a day, which is
making me tied and bringing me some relief and improvement.

Jessica and Jonathan have dealt w/my illness pretty well, although
Jessica keeps wanting me to come home home NOW and can't quite
understand why I can't. Jonathan is sorta afraid of me as I had a
tracheostomy, although we're looking to get rid of that soon. We did
all go outside on Sunday afternoon with me in my wheelchair, and Jon
was not afraid - he was thrilled - he was running around saying,
"Mommy, are you coming out?" He wanted to make sure I was going to go
outside with him. It was a good time for everyone (and my first time
outside in 3 months).

Dale has been a trooper and continues to come to the hospital every
night. Mom has been inspirational. She has continued to take care of
me and love me at times when I thought I would not make it. She's
rarely missed a day at the hospital and certainly has never missed the
opportunity to call. She's rampaged the internet looking for info on
GBS and can pass that on to you. She's become a real expert and could
become a nurse at this point.

Ron has been loving, patient and kind thru the whole ordeal. I never
see him lose his patience or temper at anyone for any reason. He is a
good role model. He supports my mother as well and allows her as much
as she needs to come up here and be with me, which is a lot!

I'm hoping that you all are doing well. I think about each and every
one of you, and I miss you. Who knows, maybe we'll se you up at the

Letter I had composed to extended family for their love and support.

Lowenstein Christin, 11:26 AM 4/5/01, Email from Erika (dictated to

Cape this summer.

Much Love,

Erika

Page 2 of the letter I had composed to extended
family for their love and support.

Copy of letter dictated by
    Erika to Jessica

3/9/00

Dear Jessica,

   I was thinking about you today + thinking about how lucky I am to have you in my life. You have such a _____ that I miss so much when I think of you, I cry. I wish I was there for you more to see you _____ listen to your problems and joys. But _____ the hospital and I can't be there _____. I go for surgery on Monday — hopefully that should help but it will still be a while before I come home. Will you take this $10 + take everyone out for ice cream to keep remembering me — (I like peanut butter parfait). So for the time being _____ _____ _____ _____ Love.

Letter composed to Jessica that Mom wrote for me.

3/9/2001

Dear Jessica,

I was thinking about you today and thinking about how lucky I am to have you in my life. You have such a gentle, loving spirit that I miss so much. When I think of you, I cry. I wish I was there for you more to see you every day and listen to your problems and joys.

But now I'm in the hospital and I can't be there every day.

I go for surgery on Monday – hopefully that should help but it will still be a while before I come home.

Will you take this $10 and take everyone out for ice cream to keep remembering me – (I like peanut buster parfait)?

So, for the time being have some ice cream and listen to Daddy, Grandma, and Grandpa and know that I love you.

All my love,

Mommy

Letter to Jessica (dictated by me; written by Mom).

copy of letter dictated by Erika to Jonathan

3/9/01

Dear Jonathan,

I heard you were calling the other morning. Here's a big kiss from mommy. You are my most favorite precious little boy, and I'm sorry you have to be without me. Hopefully soon you will understand you are so smart. Daddy brought me some of your hair. I can't want to see you. I love you very very much

Wugs & kisses,
mommy

Letter composed to Jonathan that Mom wrote for me

3/9/2001

Dear Jonathan,

I heard you were calling for me the other morning. Here's a big hug and a big kiss from Mommy. You are my most favorite, precious little boy, and I'm sorry you have to be without me.

Hopefully school is going well. I understand you moved up a level. You are so smart.

Daddy brought me some of your hair. I can't wait to see you.

I love you very, very much.

Hugs and kisses,

Mommy

Letter to Jonathan (dictated by me; written by Mom).

September 8, 2002

Dear Erika,

Well, the journal is finally finished; I think it has taken me nine months to complete it. It is 15 months today that you were discharged from Florida Hospital Rehab. I marvel at all the progress you have made.

All kinds of memories fill my mind as I reflect on this time: the first few weeks when you were home having physical therapy and frustrated having to have part-time help. I remember driving you to Kash 'n Karry on June 12 and you were annoyed that you had to ride on the motorized cart -- you only did that once! And around July 13 you called and said you passed your driver's license and had a handicapped sticker, and then the aide was gone and you were driving Jessica to ice skating! I remember telling you how scared I was, and I know now how big a step that was towards reclaiming your independence!!!

I also remember when Ron and I took you to Lake Eola Yacht Club (6/23/01) to celebrate "coming home." Afterwards we were wheeling you around the lake and came across Gloria, your R.N. in Intensive Care at ORMC. She said, "It's a miracle....all the nursing staff thought you weren't going to make it but we couldn't say anything."

If Gloria could see you the other night at karate class and then learn that you had gotten your yellow belt already, she would have said, "the miracles keep happening" and they do!

So much of what has transpired since you left the hospital has been due to your persistent dedication to a complete recovery. I remember you hiding your canes during Jonathan's birthday party a month after you came home. You said you didn't want people to think you were "handicapped."

I can't wait to see what the next year will bring, and remember, be gentle with yourself. Love those feet! They are healing as fast as they can.

It has been a privilege and honor to share your journey with you....in fact, it has been a most profound life-changing event for me. May I always remember its teachings.

Love you, always + forever,

Mom

Letter from my mom as she completed her journals. I think it was cathartic for her. It took me much longer to put pen to paper.